NERVOUS DISORDERS AND RELIGION

NERVOUS DISORDERS AND RELIGION

A Study of Souls in the Making

by

JOHN G. McKENZIE
M.A., B.D., D.D. (*Aberdeen*)
*Jesse Boot Professor of Social Science
and Psychology*

*Being the Tate Lectures
delivered in Manchester College
Oxford, in 1947*

GREENWOOD PRESS, PUBLISHERS
WESTPORT, CONNECTICUT

Library of Congress Cataloging in Publication Data

McKenzie, John Grant, 1882-
  Nervous disorders and religion.

  Reprint of the 1951 ed. published by G. Allen and
Unwin, London, which was issued as Tate lectures, 1947.
    1. Pastoral psychology--Addresses, essays, lectures.
2. Psychotherapy--Addresses, essays, lectures. I. Ti-
tle. II. Series: Tate lectures ; 1947.
BV4012.M293 1981   253.5   79-8719
ISBN 0-313-22192-8 (lib. bdg.)

BV
4012
. M293
1981

First published in 1951.

Reprinted with the permission of George Allen and
Unwin Ltd.

Reprinted from an original copy in the collection of
Fackenthal Library, Franklin and Marshall College.

Reprinted in 1981 by Greenwood Press
A division of Congressional Information Service, Inc.
88 Post Road West, Westport, Connecticut 06881

Printed in the United States of America

10 9 8 7 6 5 4 3 2 1

PREFACE

In 1944 I was honoured by the Principal and Governors of Manchester College, Oxford, by being invited to give a series of four lectures, under the Henry Tate Endowment, on psychology in relation to pastoral work. These lectures were published under the title of *Nervous Disorders and Character*. The *Tate Lectures* are delivered every three years, and in 1947 I was highly honoured by a second invitation to deliver six lectures.

This volume is the outcome of that honour.

I delayed the publication as in 1948 I was asked to deliver four lectures to the Summer School of Theology of St. Andrew's University; and I abridged the lectures delivered in Oxford in 1947. I felt sure that the final MS. for publication would benefit from the keen criticism of that theological school. I was not mistaken. In the same year I repeated the four lectures to the Iona Community, where again they were subjected to helpful criticism, especially the lecture on *Spiritual Healing*. The result of these two repetitions of the lectures was to make me expand the material. Nevertheless, substantially the lectures are as I gave them in Oxford.

A year's delay was caused by a serious illness which laid me aside for some months. Again the lectures have benefited by the extra reading of that period of forced abstention from lecturing and seeing people.

In the first two lectures I have outlined a psychological doctrine of man. Psychology is moving steadily away from the Freudian and Instinctivist concept of human nature. In other words, 'instinct' is a dying category so far as human behaviour is concerned. With the late Lloyd Morgan I am willing to concede that behaviour may have its roots in dispositions which are inherited, and such behaviour tendencies would rightly be termed 'instinctive'. But 'instincts' as defined, say by McDougall or Freud, savour too much of semi-independent entities having a sort of right of their own to be exercised or indulged. These instinctive behaviour-tendencies are evolved in the interests of fundamental bio-logical-needs of the organism and personality-needs of the Self. The emphasis today is upon the self or subject. That self or subject has a *telos* like every other organism, a *nisus* towards a person as a self-conscious harmonious whole. I believe that this *telos* is to be identified with what is called the 'image of God'; and when the *telos* is thwarted or re-pressed, a disturbance of the personality follows, although not necessarily a mental breakdown. Human nature is *Holistic,* and when that holistic tendency is thwarted, per-sonality in the true sense of the term may never develop at all.

The third lecture is concerned with the kind of conflicts within the personality that can lead to maladjusted, un-adjusted or neurotic symptoms. I had fully intended to add an extra chapter, as an appendix, on sex conflicts. I doubt, however, whether I could have said anything new. Such recent books as Kenneth Walker's *Physiology of Sex* in the Penguin series, and Dr. Schwartz' *Psychology of Sex* in the same series along with Walker's *Sex Difficulties of the Male* really cover the sex difficulties which lead to neuroticism or maladjustment. Guntripp in his *Psychology for Ministers and Social Workers* has dealt admirably, from the Christian point of view, with the sex problems of adolescence. What is wanted today by all interested in the problems of sex is a therapy for sex difficulties rather than another volume or even chapter on the diagnosis of these problems. Be that as it may, I decided not to go beyond the range I took in the original lectures.

The fourth lecture deals with the problem of the origin and dissipation of the sense of guilt; and with the conflicts which arise through the activity of the repressive, prohibitive conscience or, to give it the term used by psycho-analysts, the *super ego*. That meant dealing with the development of conscience, both negative and positive.

In the fifth lecture, I have tried to outline and, as far as possible, to valuate the various methods of mental healing from simple suggestion and re-assurance through the analytic methods to the new therapy of Counseling which is taking such a firm hold of American clinical psychologists, and concerning which there is already a formidable bibliography. A good deal of the lecture, however, is taken up with Spiritual Healing as usually understood; and I have tried to show the bearing of psycho-somatic medicine on the 'cures' claimed at Lourdes, and by Faith-healers and Christian Scientists. My experience of 'Shock' Therapies may have been unfortunate, as I have to confess that from the psychological point of view and from the point of view of a curative treatment for neurotic troubles they are like Faith-healing—a plunge in the dark.

The final lecture, like that on Spiritual Healing, has been considerably expanded. I have tried to meet some of the psychological criticisms of religion, but have been mainly concerned with the types of religion which are inimical to mental health, and the kind of religious experience in which the personality becomes free from the debilitating effects of a morbid sense of guilt, becomes unified, and receives a sense of security and that sense of *belonging* so essential to the healthy and happy mind.

I have become more and more aware that there is a fundamental difference between the *Healing of Minds* and the *Care of Souls*—a distinction well brought out in a brilliant volume to be published by Allen and Unwin on Pastoral Psychology, by a Swedish writer, Borgsten. The aims of Pastoral Psychology are much wider than those of Psychiatry or Psycho-pathology. Nevertheless, if the pastor and social worker or the counsellor is to help needy personalities, maladjusted and unadjusted individuals, they will need all the help that psychiatry and psycho-pathology can give; but they should not forget that an intelligent and well-informed religious experience is still the greatest and quickest resolver of the conflicts which press upon the soul of man in this modern age of ours.

It only remains for me to express again my gratitude to the Principal and Governors of Manchester College, Oxford, for the great honour they conferred on me by giving me the opportunity in the two succeeding series of Tate Lectures to gather up what I believe will be helpful to all pastors who care for the souls of their people.

To Principal and Mrs. Cross I owe a real debt of gratitude for the hospitality of their home; and it was with sincere regret and sorrow that I learned of the Principal's enforced retirement through illness. To Dr. McLachlan, the Acting-Principal, and Professor Williams, as well as the students, I am grateful for the welcome they gave me and the appreciative manner in which they received the lectures. I owe not a little to their questions.

I am under a great debt to my friend, Rev. K. M. Hamilton, M.A., B.D., of Wallington, Surrey, one of our brilliant young ministers, for the great care with which he read the MS., and the suggestions he made both as to matter and style. My thanks are also due to my daughter, Margaret Laws, M.A., M.B., Ch.B., and her husband, Frederic Laws, M.B., B.S., for reading the proofs. To the latter I owe the reference to psycho-somatic factors in tuberculosis.

As far as I know I have acknowledged in footnotes all the quotations I have made; and I owe thanks to the Editor of the *Expository Times* for his permission to use material of two articles which at his request I wrote for that monthly periodical.

JOHN G. McKENZIE

Paton College,
Nottingham.

CONTENTS

LECTURE 1

WHAT IS ORIGINAL HUMAN NATURE ?

GLANCING over the psychology book-shelves recently I was struck by the titles of publications by medical psychologists. If we did not know that the writers were medical men we might easily come to the conclusion that sermons were again appealing to a large public. *The Triumphant Spirit* might on a hasty view be expected to be a new volume of sermons by A. J. Gossip instead of a volume dealing with nervous troubles by Dr. Graham Howe. *The Human Approach* suggests a companion volume to Dr. Jack's *From the Human End* and certainly not an introduction to psychological medicine by Dr. H. Yellowlees. *Our Inner Conflicts* has an evangelical sound though it is written by that acute observer of human character-trends, Karen Horney. Even Jung's *Modern Man in Search of a Soul* would not by the laws of the association of ideas suggest a series of studies on various aspects of psychotherapy.

And it is not merely in their titles that these doctors suggest the closeness of their work to pastoral psychology or preaching, but also their matter. For their subject-matter deals with the problems which ministers, teachers and social workers meet every day. Not a little of what they write could be material for next Sunday's sermon. Perhaps they give us a hint as to how the pulpit can regain its ancient power. Should not a great many of our sermons approximate to public psycho-therapeutic guidance—an unravelling of the soul's conflicts, a strengthening of the will to meet the temptations of life, a deepening of the philosophy of life, or the faith by which a man meets the contradictions of life? There is a need in every one of us for a sense of spiritual security. There have been periods in Church History when the sense of spiritual security was disturbed by changes in the intellectual outlook, and the great preachers directed their message so as to strengthen the rational grounds of Christian Faith. There will always be a place for such preaching. Just because 'the heart has reasons which the reason knows not of' the two have somehow to be reconciled, and indeed Pascal's work was to reconcile the two. In our own day the lack of the sense of spiritual security is due to many things, but not least to the absence of authoritative spiritual and moral guidance. This spiritual and moral guidance has been the age-long task of the Church ; and now that the Church is failing to give it there is feverish activity among educational spokesmen to fill the gap. One has only to read such volumes as Sir Richard Livingstone's *Education for a World Adrift,* or his recent *Task of Education* to find that educationists are as much at sea as to what should be taught as the Church.

Our interest lies, however, in the neurotic conflicts which are the result of this lack of spiritual and moral guidance. Somehow the Church must regain its power to deal with the inner difficulties of both young and old so as to give them a sense of spiritual and moral security. 'We know not whither Thou goest and how can we know the way?' asked Thomas of our Lord. How can we take the way if we know not whither it leads? Even when the moral end is known and accepted our instinctive inclinations have to be brought into harmony with it; and that is seldom done without a good deal of psychological conflict. Hence the need for preachers, pastors, social workers, educationalists and doctors to know something of the anatomy of the soul: its organs, its conflicts, it diseases. Only then will the sermon or the moral lessons in the school approximate to psychotherapeutic guidance.

So far as the minister or clergyman is concerned this will necessitate a modification of the theological curriculum.[1] Although no less emphasis would be laid upon the strictly theological and exegetical disciplines a new emphasis would be laid upon the fact that as ministers we are expected to be able to deal with the soul in all its activities. The intellectual difficulties of our people we must be able to meet; our congregations need to be grounded in their religious faith and ethical standards; our young adolescents must learn something of the basic religious experiences if they are to be able to meet and interpret their own inner experiences. Karl Mannheim[2] has some brilliant pages in which he shows the tremendous sociological importance of these basic religious experiences both for society and the individual. What we must remember is that the Church lives not in virtue of the infallibility of her creed, or the nature of her church organisation, but by the capacity of her ministers and teachers to elicit the moral and spiritual experiences in which her members find their inner conflicts resolved, and their way of life made clear. That ancient power is still hers if she avails herself of the knowledge laboriously built up by workers in the various fields of psychology. She must not only know God; she must also know human nature. Indeed there is no greater source for knowledge of human nature than the Bible, but it needs a psychological interpretation as well as a theological. When a medical psychologist 'cures' a case of neurotic conflict it is in virtue, not of the application of medical science,

---

[1] Cf. Brunner's Essay in the Volume 'The Predicament of the Church'. p. 82 ff.

[2] See p. 131 ff. 'The Diagnosis of our Time'.

but of his knowledge of human nature and its conflicts within the individual's conscience.

nowledge of Human Nature

To understand the problems of human break-down and their relation to religion we must have a knowledge of human nature. Alas! it is one of those subjects to which Bernard Shaw's dictum really applies: 'Though everybody nowadays seems to know the x y z of everything nobody knows the a b c of anything'.[1] The little that we do know about human nature and its conflicts is infinitesimal in comparison with our ignorance. Nevertheless, there is no subject where people take their knowledge so much for granted as in the case of human nature.

One writer,[2] Professor Hocking, tells us that there are three questions which everyone engaged in making or remaking man should ask:

1. What is original human nature?

2. What do we want to make of it?

3. How far is it possible to make of it what we wish?

Here there is the assumption that there is an original, fixed basis of human nature, apparently plastic enough for someone to attempt to make of it what he will, yet resistant enough to refuse to be made into something inconsistent with the original basis. There can be no question of the relevancy of these questions. Conflict begins when someone tries to make a child into something the child was never intended to become; or attempts to bend the individual irrespective of the wishes of the unfortunate victim.

An illustration will help us here. A young married

[1] Quoted by Sir Richard Livingstone in 'The Task of Education'.
[2] 'Human Nature and its Re-making,' p. 5.

woman developed an acute anxiety condition. Her husband was rather easy-going but he was an excellent father and truly affectionate towards his wife. Analysis quickly showed that she was resisting the influence of a dominating mother. The latter was against her daughter marrying at all; advised her against having any children. After the birth of her first child the mother 'dared' her to have any more. About eighteen months after her second child an acute anxiety-state developed. During this state the patient committed an extremely interesting symbolic act. She pawned her engagement ring, and went and bought a pair of shoes that she did not need. The pawning of the ring could not have been done in order to buy the shoes, for she neither needed the shoes nor was she without money. The act showed the extreme conflict between the resentment of her mother and her love for her husband; and also the attempt to push the whole conflict into the unconscious. The pawning of her engagement ring was the symbolic attempt to revert to a state of mind before her engagement; the buying of the shoes was a clear repudiation of the mother. She had never been allowed to buy anything for herself; her mother chose and bought her clothes and shoes. The act symbolically rid her of husband and mother—the two elements in her unconscious conflict. When she was getting well she recalled that just before her breakdown she felt a tremendous urge for another baby and the fear of what her mother would say. The whole trouble was caused by the dominating mother attempting to shape the daughter's life according to her wishes and completely against the wishes of the patient.

The relevancy of Professor Hocking's third question about making human nature what it was never intended to become can be seen in abundance in Professor James' chapter on

'Saintliness' in his 'Varieties of Religious Experience.' It is truly sad reading ; and the effect upon a healthy mind is that if this is saintliness then we had better have as little of it as possible. Yet the method is perfectly simple. You just steadily deny yourself until all desire has vanished into the unconscious. The psychotherapist sees the 'saintly' type as a patient suffering from a neurotic need for perfection. Such patients are compelled to be a hundred-per-cent. perfect. They are driven relentlessly by a rigid standard of morals, and dare not deviate one inch from it. They get no joy out of their moral achievements, but fall into dreadful misery if they come short. Actually there is no love for the good, but just a fear of wrong-doing. They blame themselves for every untoward thing that happens to them, irrespective of the external circumstances. They are seldom free from guilt-feelings; their holiness is an unhappy holiness; for they cannot refrain from finding flaws in themselves, and dread any reproaches by other people. Moral scruples hedge them in until they can scarcely do anything without some kind of doubt. Their perfectionism is not the outcome of spontaneous desire but a compulsion-neurosis.

We must return to Professor Hocking's first question : *What is original human nature?* The assumption here is that there is some kind of fixed basis. Two other writers, however, who have given a great deal of study to the subject assure us that 'Human nature is not something that exists at birth. Neither is it a set of biological traits or tendencies which unfold or mature after birth. It is rather an acquired nature which represents the modelling of the plastic, unorganised part of man's native equipment. The modelling of this plastic original nature takes place in social experience, and results in the development of such forms of behaviour which we may term social habits, attitudes, sentiments, self-control'.[1] Their judgment is contained in a quotation they make from another writer: 'Man is not born human. It is only slowly and laboriously, in fruitful contact and co-operation with his fellows, that he attains the distinctive qualities of human nature'.[2]

In other words, man, as personality, is not ready-made; he is not the outcome of the interplay of a set of separate instincts nor the push of libido for expression, nor of a series of conditioned reflexes. Human nature in these writers is not a *biological* term at all; it is a *moral* term actually defining a standard of character that is reached in fruitful contact and co-operation with one's fellows.

The position is really a protest against the concept of human nature as a bundle of instincts, or conditioned reflexes. In answer to his own question Professor Hocking seems to think this is truly answered by listing a catalogue of instincts and emotions after McDougall and Thorndike. He is careful, however, to remind us that satisfaction is peculiar to a mind, and that it is nonsensical to speak of a satisfied instinct. (Actually it is a self that is satisfied and neither an instinct nor a mind.) As Dr. Hocking has well put it: 'The word "instinct" has no magic to annul the obvious truth that satisfaction is a state of mind, nor to evade the long labour of experience in determining what can satisfy a mind. Conscious life is engaged quite as much *in trying to find out what it wants* as in trying to get it.[3]

The present position is that apart from medical psychologists no psychologist of note contends that a catalogue of instincts nor for that matter reflexes capable of being con-

---

[1] 'Social Psychology,' by Krueger and Reckless, p. 27.
   Cf. also 'The Person and the Common Good,' by Maritain, p. 31 ff.
[2] 'Social Psychology,' by Krueger and Reckless, p. 27 f.
[3] 'Human Nature and its Re-making,' preface.

ditioned will give us original human nature. 'Instincts . . . is a diminishing category in higher animal forms especially in the human'.[1] That we start with some kind of biological equipment in the form of needs and behaviour-mechanisms no one could possibly deny, e.g., the sucking reflex and the tendency to sleep when we are fatigued. Outside a few be-haviour-mechanisms such as swallowing, breathing, walk-ing, excretion, and nutrition, there is not a great deal of our behaviour that is uniform. Certainly we can all laugh, but not necessarily at the same stories; we can all experience anger, but not at the same causes; we can all experience fear, but not in the same situations or at the same objects; we can all be curious or pugnacious, but not necessarily *about the same things*.

Man is always a particular being with an individuality that cannot be ignored. That is why he eludes science, even psychological science.[2] General psychology treats *mind in general, the nature of man in general, behaviour tendencies in general*. You cannot treat people *in general*. Science as such sees each individual thing as a member of a class, or an instance of a universal principle. But each human indi-vidual is unique! He is a never-repeated phenomenon, act-ing and thinking and feeling in a way peculiar to himself. He thus evades the normal procedure of science. When we have abstracted all that is general in the individual human being, we are left with what has been called 'an insoluble residue in the background which differentiates not only the genius from the common man, but the day-labourer from the day-labourer'.[3] It is in this background we must look

---

[1] Quoted by Erich Fromm in 'The Fear of Freedom', p. 26.

[2] Cf. The volume in the International Library, 'Psychology of Intelligence and Will,' Wyatt, pp. 133—136.

[3] 'Psychology of Christian Soul,' Stevens, Chapter 1.

for those ultimate attitudes the individual takes to life, determining one towards an æsthetic attitude, another towards an ethical, and still another towards a spiritual attitude. Individuality is not to be identified with temperament, for temperament is not unique. It is not talent, though it may determine the line along which the talent will be used; it is not character, though that seems to have a determining effect. It is this individuality which defies all our 'plans of salvation,' and all our mass production systems of education. It is in virtue of this unique element, I believe, that we begin to select the experiences which we shall weave into our personality. It certainly has a determining effect as to how we shall react to our experiences.

I introduce this factor in human nature not because I can explain it; it is an element in the ultimate basis of human nature with which we start out to acquire a personality. In little children individuality is as a rule conspicuous; in the genius and the elite it is dynamic and obvious.

Leaving aside the problem of individuality, let us get at the core of this nature with which we set out on the journey towards becoming a human being, the basic original nature that determines our direction towards human nature. In other words we must attempt to probe into the springs of behaviour. These springs are dynamic; it is when their force is impeded that conflict arises. We break down in resisting some forceful element in our make-up.

The Doctrine of Fundamental Needs

I find that the best way to conceive the dynamic core of our nature, with which we all start out on the enterprise of gaining a personality, can be expressed best in terms of *Needs*—needs which are the same wherever we find developed human beings. These needs give rise to behaviour-

tendencies which are infinitely varied in different individuals. No two individuals react in the same way to the
same psychological situation. Some of these needs we share
with the animals, others are peculiarly human, and it is the
latter which determine what we may call purely human behaviour. It is in the dynamic striving to satisfy these needs
that we are compelled to enter into fruitful contact and cooperation with our fellows, and the manner in which
we strive determines, consciously or unconsciously, our
behaviour-tendencies, our relations to our social environment, our relations to others and the degree of harmony
within our own souls.

The biological needs I can only mention briefly. Their
importance for personality lies in the fact that they can
become personal ends, and our mode of satisfying them
comes within the sphere of moral conduct. The manner in
which we strive to satisfy these needs may give rise to moral
and psychological conflicts, e.g., a perversion.

1. First there is the *Biological Need to Preserve the
Organism.* It is in the interest of this need that there have
been evolved the appetites of hunger and thirst and the
physiological functions of nutrition and excretion. But the
body needs rest and recuperation, hence the tendency to
sleep when we are fatigued. Danger may come to the organism from the natural elements, hence the tendency to provide for ourselves shelter from the extremes of weather.
Any threat to the organism tends to arouse fear, and
Rivers[1] has listed no less than five possible reactions to
bodily danger. All these behaviour-tendencies involve the
intellectual functions. Through them we learn to differentiate between the values of various foods and drinks and to
modify the manner in which we shall provide for the bodily

---

[1] 'Instinct and The Unconscious.'

needs and the safety of the organism. Health may become a positive ideal; cleanliness, culinary arts, bodily fitness may produce entirely acquired behaviour-tendencies. The purely biological need may thus become the basis of a highly-prized moral and personal end. The natural 'wants', as T. H. Green[1] pointed out, imply 'wanted objects' and these 'wanted objects' may become more important than the wants themselves. It is when the 'wanted object' is incompatible with other ends of the personality that conflict arises. Green gives the illustration of Esau selling his birthright for a mess of pottage. Here the 'want' is the hunger which any kind of food could have satisfied, the mess of pottage, that for which he was willing to sell his birthright. Two, at least, of 'the deadly sins' are connected with this biological need to preserve the organism, namely gluttony and sloth.

Psychologically, conflicts are not uncommon even at this level of biological needs. The need to preserve the organism may come into conflict with the purely personal end of keeping the figure slim, and we may get a severe neurosis called 'anorexia nervosa'. A young girl seems full of energy; she will walk or run for miles. But there is a pathological refusal to eat. There is no bodily disease, but naturally there is always the possibility of the resistance to disease becoming so low that severe physical illness may occur. In this particular case, the girl felt she was getting too fat, and simply refused to eat. The trouble may also occur in girls who do not want to grow up. Such cases are always best under institutional treatment as the appetite must be restored and weight increased if permanent damage is to be prevented.

The conflicts and neuroses common to war-time are

[1] 'Prolegomena to Ethics.'

often the outcome of the need to preserve the organism coming into conflict with personal ends. A young soldier wants to preserve his organism and yet there is the personal end of being respected by others. Only in so far as he courageously fulfils his duty can the personal end be realised.

An interesting case of this kind was a young member of the Air Force. He broke down with physical symptoms for which no physical basis could be found. I undertook a deep analysis. He volunteered at the request of army headquarters from a regiment in which he had risen to the position of sergeant. No sooner was he posted to Canada than his symptoms began to appear. While training there were some accidents in which he saw a number of his fellow-trainees killed. He passed his examinations, received his wings, but the symptoms increased in intensity until finally, after some time under a psychiatrist, he was posted to a corps at home in which there was little or no chance of incurring danger; and although the symptoms caused him a great deal of discomfort they were not severe enough to merit his discharge.

Analysis showed that he volunteered because all the others in his first regiment to whom appeal had been made had done so, and he did not care to be the odd man out. While undergoing training he was repeatedly pulled up by his teachers for lack of concentration, and was actually expected to fail. Through a dream we got back to conflict in his mind that had been entirely repressed. Before his examination he 'wondered' whether it would not be better to do badly in the examination and thus get out of the Air Force. He is a very intelligent man, and he knew he could pass, and his pride came to his aid here, and he determined to pass in order to show his teachers that he was no fool. Actually he came out of the examination with a very high place, to the astonishment of his teachers. His pride was satisfied but there was no real elation; and his symptoms increased, for there was no valid reason why he should not go out on bombing expeditions over Germany. Fundamentally his fear was of a situation where he had no chance to save himself as would occur if his bombing plane were hit from either the ground or an enemy fighter. He was too proud to acknowledge his fear and be thought a coward even to himself. He repressed his conflict and was thus able to display his wings without having to face danger, and he was able to maintain his pride—the pride that would not allow him to do badly in his examination—by persuading himself that had it not been for his symptoms he would have been operating over Germany. Actually, as we can see, his symptoms were produced to preserve his organism when the danger to it came up against the personal end to be well thought of by others.

I have said enough to show that so prominent a biological need can come into conflict with what are personal ends, which may give rise to severe conflicts and neuroses.

2. The second biological need with which we start our journey towards becoming a full human being is the *Need to Reproduce our Kind*. Here we have the physiological appetite of sex, the behaviour-mechanism of copulation, the process of gestation, the reflex action of the birth process, and the feeding and weaning of the child. Then, there are all the behaviour-tendencies by which we woo and win the mate. Probably it is here more than in any other of our natural needs that we realise how varied behaviour-tendencies can be, although they are correlated with the same fundamental need. The behaviour-tendencies associated with wooing and mating vary according to the period in which we are born and the cultural standards

of our community. They vary from hitting the girl on the head and carrying her away, to bending humbly before a Victorian father and begging for his daughter's hand. Hence we can see how unintelligible it is to speak of a separate instinct to woo the mate if we desire to convey some information about the manner in which we win a mate. That behaviour varies enormously even in modern life. To win a mate may be the spring behind all kinds of achievement on the part of a male as it certainly is behind the very colour of the lipstick a young girl uses.

Its interest for us lies in the fact that it becomes a very personal end in man. As a matter of fact the need itself may be ignored and subordinated entirely to the individual's personal pleasure. The pleasure which the behaviour-tendencies connected with this need evoke may be the sole motive of sexual activity—the biological need and the sociological purpose entirely ignored. No psychotherapist or social worker can afford to neglect the connection between this need and its frustration and anxiety-states, or its repression and other severe forms of both neurosis and psychosis. Maternity is a need in woman much more than sexual satisfaction is a need in man: and the control of birth has real psychological dangers for her. Also the maternal need drives a woman (often unconsciously) much more than any desire for sexual satisfaction. If the satisfaction of the maternal need is frustrated by the selfishness of the husband, it nearly always has painful results. That we can leave until I come to deal with our inner conflicts.

3. We come now to what I call *Personality Needs*. They are peculiarly human and are not shared by the animals. Without them there could be no human nature. It is in striving to satisfy these personality-needs that human nature is acquired and character achieved. It is they which give

meaning to our strivings, our behaviour-tendencies, and indeed to all the higher ends we pursue.

They must not, however, be considered in isolation. They develop against a social background, in a system of personal relations; and they are satisfied within a sociological field.[1] Nevertheless, they involve a self-conscious individual who is striving to realise himself. It is this self-conscious individual who transforms purely biological needs into personal ends that subserve the personality rather than the organism. It is this self-conscious individual who experiences anxiety-states, obsessive fears, compulsion-states, depression-states. Just because the individual is self-conscious every situation is evaluated in relation to himself. It is this fact of selfhood that makes nonsense of all our attempts to explain man purely on biological or neurological grounds. To those who interpret man mainly in terms of biology, human breakdown occurs when some primary instinct is frustrated. On the view I am presenting of human nature, the individual breaks down because there is a threat to the integrity of the self, or to some dominant interest of the self. The biologists think in terms of separate instincts, each apparently semi-independent, and in terms of specific emotions which apparently are the same for everyone, so also do the behaviourists and physiologists. Because they ignore the self who experiences the emotions they speak as if the emotions have the same texture irrespective of the situation in which the emotion is aroused. The behaviourists are right when they contend that a child experiences fear if it loses the sense of physical security, or when it is suddenly dropped. But the fear an individual experiences at the thought of being 'dropped' by his companions is a completely different

---

[1] Cf. 'The Person and the Common Good,' by Maritain, p. 34.

emotion. It may be, as James thought, that the physical concomitants of emotion are always the same, but we must not infer from this that the psychological texture of the emotion is always the same. The fear of losing a game of billiards is very different from the fear of losing one's job; and the latter fear is very different from the fear of death. It is the *meaning* of a situation to a self-conscious individual that gives the feeling tone of the emotion. It is probable that purely organic fear arising out of some threat to the organism is texturally always the same, although even here there would be shades of difference due to self-conscious thought. But the threat to the moral integrity of the individual by some behaviour-tendency within the individual is a different fear from that which arises with the threat to his organic existence by a malignant growth. Dr. Hadfield[1] has remarked that the behaviour of patients in a surgical ward suffering from some real threat to their organic existence differs from that of patients in a psychological ward, whose anxiety-state contains a fear that they have a malignant growth. The surgical cases are mostly asleep, or lying quietly; whereas the psychological cases are sleepless or restless. The latter's threat is to the integrity of their personality. We must recognise that in all psychological difficulties it is a self that is disturbed, and not an instinct. If, like Freud, we think of a psychological disturbance as due to frustration, we must remember that it is the self that is disturbed by the psychological consequences of the frustration. If, e.g., a married woman felt frustrated because her husband was either unwilling or refused to give her a baby, there would be no breakdown; but if subconsciously she began to 'wish' that she had married someone else, or played with the idea of coitus with another man and re-

---

[1] 'Psychology and Morals,' Chapter 1.

pressed the tendency to do so, she would develop a neurosis. It is thus not the frustration that is the causative factor, but the repression of the tendency offering a threat to her moral integrity.

1. It is from phenomena such as these that we learn the most fundamental need of personality. *It is the Need to Realise the Personality as a Harmonious Whole both in its inner and outer relations.* Original human nature has a *need* to develop so that conscience, behaviour-tendencies, emotions and thought will be in harmony. Experience must harmonise with feeling, as Hobhouse[1] puts it. Personal relations with others will be found to be as important for mental health as the unity of inner relations.

Not only so, but the self must be in harmonious relations with its biological needs. In other words, the self must unify with its own moral ends the behaviour-tendencies associated with the satisfaction of biological needs; it must permeate them so that they become subservient to the ends of personality. *Human breakdown is the outcome of the failure of the self to unify its own dynamic tendencies with the ends of personality.* We shall see later that this definition covers the inability of the self to integrate its experiences. Whenever there is this failure or inability, the self is frustrated; it is unable to integrate either its experience or its behaviour-tendencies. The result is a 'complex' or a character-neurosis. In the reaction to that failure the self becomes maladjusted or distorted or simply fails to realise happiness.

Just as to how all this works out we must leave to the remaining lectures. At the moment I am concerned to impress upon your minds that the causes of breakdown must

---

[1] 'The Rational Good,' p. 77. (London: George Allen & Unwin Ltd.)

be looked for in the self, in the need of the self to realise itself as a whole, in the need to express the unity of self-consciousness in the unity of behaviour-tendencies which are in harmony with conscience, emotion and rational thought. *It is a self that breaks down;* and until psychologists realise that disabling symptoms come from a self frustrated by its own weakness not much progress is going to be made either in prevention or cure of the neuroses. Underlying Dr. H. Yellowlees' emphasis in his lectures to medical students on 'The Human Approach' to their future patients there is a tacit assumption of a self, a self that is suffering, anxious, afraid. There is a good deal of emphasis on the part of psychotherapists at the present time on the necessity to help their patients to face the moral issues involved in their neurosis. Dr. Karen Horney in her latest volume, *Our Inner Conflicts,* urges that we can no longer avoid facing moral issues with our patients. Dr. Culpin admits, although deprecating any tendency on the part of the practitioner to allow his moral judgments to play any part while investigating the causes of some delinquency or breakdown, that 'when the need arises the moral aspect can be presented as a study of cause and effect, in which the obligations to the society in which we live must receive the first consideration'.[1]

It is not irrelevant to mention that probably ninety-percent. of patients blame themselves morally. Actually a good deal of one's treatment consists in alleviating the harshness of their moral self-condemnation and moral judgments upon themselves. Their intuition, however, of moral weakness should not be ignored. Often they are as weak as they think themselves, and not seldom there are real unconscious

---

[1] 'Psychology in General Practice,' edited by Alan Moncrieff, p. 10.

causes for feeling morally afraid and blameworthy. Two illustrations will help us here. The patient was a married woman who suffered from the fear of collapsing in the street. She dare not stop in the centre of the city if she went out shopping, nor could she stand in a queue. Her marriage was not satisfactory, her husband being mean and obsessed with the idea of making money. The woman was very much above the average in intelligence, and her initiative was the mainspring of a flourishing business. Her need for affection was unsatisfied. The root of her trouble was found in the fact that she had met accidentally when she was down town and in perfect health an old sweetheart who had to give her up because another girl had become pregnant by him. He invited her to coffee, and as she was leaving him asked her to meet him again, a request which she refused. Actually her affection for this man needed a very little spark to be relit. Unconsciously she wished that she could accidentally come across him again, and found herself thinking oftener of him when she went down town than was comfortable for her sense of loyalty to her husband. She repressed the wish to see him, and her symptoms were her defence reaction against meeting him again. She confessed that she was not at all sure of how she would react if the said old sweetheart were to take her out and make advances in the way of love-making. She was really guarding herself against a moral weakness which became perfectly conscious as she was cured of her fears.[1]

More enlightening still is the case of a man whose trouble began in an experience of uncomfortable feelings at a Masonic Meeting. He then began to feel apprehensive in his club and at race meetings until he tended to experience the feelings whenever he went out. At first he found that if he

[1] Cf. 'The Distressed Mind,' in 'The Thinker's Library,' p. 137.

took some whisky or gin the feelings disappeared as by magic, and he would 'feel fine'. Greater and greater amounts were needed to numb the feelings. This, however, created a new fear. Instead of 'feeling fine' he began to experience hostility; he looked for an argument which tended to end in a scene. Two such scenes in his club and he began to be afraid to go out at all.

The man's dreams showed that he had violated his conscience in some way. It was then found that the violation was in respect of the relations between white Europeans and black women. Both his home and church training in a British Dominion had given him a rooted disgust of any sexual relations between sexes of different colour. He remembered distinctly when he went to the British Colony to work, the horrible feeling of disgust he experienced when he saw the free relations between white Europeans and the coloured women. Nevertheless, he was persuaded, in spite of the inhibitions arising from the deeply-rooted taboo, to be like others and have his mistress. The result was that the feelings originally felt in regard to what others did were now unconsciously turned against himself. The self-criticism, which came up repeatedly in his dreams, was felt in the presence of others. The drink loosed the hostile feelings against himself but displaced them upon others. Hence he was afraid unconsciously both of temptations to continue breaking the taboo, and of the hostility which got him into trouble with members of his club. His fear of going out alone, his apprehensiveness when with others were self-defence reactions both against his temptations, his self-criticism and his hostility. There was no harmony between his experience of these coloured women and his conscience. The drive of the self towards a harmonious whole had been frustrated by his behaviour-tendencies; the integrity of the self was in danger. His breakdown was the unconscious attempt to preserve whatever degree of unity was left in the self. The self refused to integrate behaviour-tendencies which were wholly alien to the character he had built up. The moral issues had to be faced before he became free from his neurosis. Here, as in so many cases, the psychological conflict was disguising a moral conflict.

Both these cases illustrate the fact that the self *will have* wholeness. There is a need, a dynamic need, within the self to realise itself as a harmonious whole. When that is thwarted either by some experience which the self has not been able to integrate or behaviour-tendencies which threaten the integrity of the self, the danger of breakdown is present.

This need of the self to realise itself as a whole is just a particular instance of a principle running through the whole of organic nature. It is the nature of all wholes to realise themselves as wholes.[1] The organism reveals this tendency at all levels. The capacity of some of the lower animals to regrow non-vital parts which have been lost either by accident or fight is a commonplace. Even a better example is that of the split germ growing into two whole-similar twins. This characteristic of organic life shows itself as a *need* in self-conscious individuals. The very consciousness of a divided heart, of the flesh warring against the spirit and the spirit against the flesh is a real psychological proof of the *need;* for only a drive or need for unity could make us conscious of division.

The Will

It is from this need of the personality to realise itself as a harmonious whole that we get the meaning of Will as

---

[1] Cf. Smuts' 'Holism and Evolution'.

contrasted with *conation.* The latter is a general tendency characteristic both of instinctive and mental processes. Hunger is correlated with the conative tendency to seek food; thought tends to persist. Conation is active impulse; Will is directed by intelligence.[1] Conation is initiated by some bodily need or some instinctive tendency; Volition is initiated by the self—*the self is a cause.* I should define Will as *the capacity of the self to canalise its energy along the line of consciously chosen ends, and to inhibit itself from acting on impulse alone, especially if the impulsive action is not in harmony with conscience.* Will always involves intelligence. It is true that in conation we experience effort; but in Will or Volition we experience the self initiating the effort. If the self is weak in this capacity, the character is weak. It is the weakness in this capacity that every neurotic acknowledges. In an acute anxiety-state a great deal of conative energy is expended, but to no purpose; it is not correlated with intelligence. When this capacity is weak the self is open to all sorts of conflicts which may lead to abandonment of the achievement of personality altogether; or being unable to direct its behaviour-tendencies by the knowledge of good and evil, may escape into neurotic illness.

Will, then, is the activity of the self as a whole. This is a very different proposition from that made by many psychologists that Will is the activity of the whole self. As a matter of psychological fact when the Will acts it is to inhibit impulse; consequently it cannot be the activity of the whole self, for the impulse is part of that sum total we call the whole self. The *self as a whole* must be differentiated from *the whole self;* the self as a whole is conscious of itself as

[1] See the excellent volume, 'The Psychology of Intelligence and Will,' by Wyatt, in 'The International Library of Philosophy and Scientific Method'.

an entity; and it is conscious of the entities which make up the whole self. My impulses are mine but they are not me; my emotions are mine but they are not me.

The self as a whole is to the whole self as life is to the organism. The organism is not merely the sum of its organs; it is the organs animated by life. It is the self as a whole which expresses itself in Will or Volition. It is the unifying principle of our psychical make-up. Impulse is blind; it is not conscious of its own end; Will is intelligent; it is the self exercising its intelligence on the direction of impulse. When we speak of a conflict of impulses we are apt to forget we are using a figure of speech; a conflict results when inclination is opposed by Will. Here is the ground for the statement of the late Professor Laird,[1] that sentiment can only incline or solicit, it cannot govern; government is the task of the self through Volition. If the self is too weak to govern, then it may resort to repression, and there is the breakdown. It is a self that breaks down; the Will cannot canalise its energy along the line of conscious ends; but repression itself is an attempt on the part of the self to inhibit the offending behaviour-tendency.

The Will in relation to nervous disorders would need a series of lectures; the whole psychology of moral action is involved. Here I have to be satisfied by indicating my position, and leaving to some future occasion a full discussion of what I believe to be a problem that neither psychologist nor moral philosopher can ignore. The assumption of the moral philosopher is that the self can shape and govern its behaviour; the psychotherapist has to deal with people—not necessarily neurotic people—who find the task of self-

[1] 'A Study in Moral Theory,' p. 138. (London: George Allen & Unwin Ltd.)

Also Cf. Collingwood, 'Principles of Art', pp. 206—211.

government impossible. The pervert, for instance, is not necessarily a neurotic, but he is unable to direct his impulses by his Will. He may be able to inhibit his impulses from exercising themselves in action—and many of them can do this—but he is unable to direct them to normal ends. The neurotic has given up the task of self-government.

Let me now summarise as briefly as I can the position we have reached. We found that psychotherapy deals with problems essentially the same as those of the teacher, social worker or minister, in other words they deal with problems of personality. To understand these problems we were compelled to get some understanding of human nature, or rather with the original equipment with which we start on what Emerson called 'the great enterprise of realising a personality'. We dismissed the contention that the original equipment is no more than a catalogue of instincts or a list of conditioned or unconditioned reflexes. Rather, original human nature consists of certain fundamental needs and behaviour-tendencies designed to fulfil these needs. We have biological needs in common with the animals such as the *Need to Preserve the Organism,* and the *Need to Reproduce our Kind,* and with them we have the appetites and behaviour-tendencies which have been evolved to subserve these needs. In man these needs become personal ends, and as such may conflict with personality-needs. Turning from these we found that we had to keep in mind the uniqueness of each individual, or individuality through which each one of us reacts to the world differently, even in the same situation, from anyone else. Coming to personality-needs we studied the most profound need of the individual, the need of the individual to realise himself as a self-conscious harmonious whole. It is when this is frustrated that the possibility of nervous breakdown arises. To realise this harmonious whole the self must have the capacity to canalise its energy in opposition to impulse or inclination; in other words, the self must have the power of Volition or Will. Thus our psychological problems are really personality-problems, they are moral questions. The *problem* of human breakdown is really a personality-*problem*.

WHAT IS ORIGINAL HUMAN NATURE?
(Continued)

WE have seen that the most profound need of personality
is that the individual should realise himself as a harmonious
whole. That means that there is 'a prospective aim of
personality',[1] or as Hadfield calls it, 'an urge to completeness'.[2] There is, as a matter of fact, a prospective aim in
every living organism, an urge to completeness of the particular kind of organism implicit in the seed. Whether the
seed will realise its prospective aim, or completeness, is
conditioned to some extent by the environment, but by no
means wholly. Even vegetable seeds will strive to make the
most of a poor environment. The soil is necessary to the
seed; the climbing plant spontaneously feels for something
on which it can climb; the tropical plant needs shelter from
cold winds. The higher we reach in the biological scale the
less dependent is the organism upon the environment. Nevertheless, every living thing has its necessary conditions which
we can translate into needs. The seed needs the soil, and it
seeks its nourishment from it. There is a dynamic response
to conditions. So the personality-need to realise itself as a
whole has its necessary conditions. It seeks for the conditions in which its prospective aim can be realised. In men
these needs are conscious, and can be sought; difficulties in
attaining to their satisfaction can be overcome consciously.
It is these needs in the satisfaction of which the personality
as a whole is realised that we must now study.

---

[1] 'The Re-creating of the Individual,' by Beatrice Hinkle, p. 44.
[2] 'Psychology and Morals,' Hadfield, Chapter 8.

1. The first of these is the *Need for Affection*. This is the need to love and be loved. It is obvious from the biological point of view that the infant needs care. The love which a child needs is even more important from the point of view of personality-needs or the realising of human nature. There is no such thing as an isolated human being; communal[1] life, personal relations are absolutely necessary if the personality is to be realised as a whole. It is in communal life and personal relationships that the distinctively human nature is elicited and grows; and it is in personal relationships that happiness is experienced. If we define happiness as a self realising itself as a whole in contrast to pleasure, which is a satisfied impulse or desire, we can see at once the need for affection. Happiness is a satisfied self, and no self can be satisfied if personal relationships are disturbed or withheld. Affection is the bond of personal relationships. It gives the child the sense of security in its relations with others; as the child's affection is accepted by others, the child acquires spontaneity in its relations with others. The affection the child *needs* is not necessarily the kind of love a child *wants*. The love it needs is that kind of love which is based on the good of the child in the long run, and behaviour towards a child should be based on the good of the child in the long run. Not a little *mother-love* is *smother-love,* as an American put it; the result is the spoilt child who is never able to adjust itself to the conditions of happy personal relations in adult life. Such a child expects to be treated and evaluated by others as his mother treated and evaluated him. Naturally he does not receive this treatment, nor is he likely to be thought a genius; he quickly senses that he is really treated as a spoilt child and tends to develop inferiority feelings; or he may react by an unconscious

---

[1] Cf. 'The Person and the Common Good,' by Maritain, p. 34 f.

demand to be treated on the valuation of himself created by his mother's foolish treatment of him. He gets an inflated image of himself and demands to be treated as though this inflated image were a true reflection of his personality. Finding he is not so treated, he nurses his resentment and becomes unsocial.

The love which a child requires as a condition of its personality-development is always inspired by the good of the child in the long run; its demonstrative signs should not be niggardly, and yet should not be fussy.

Even more important still, according to Dr. Ian Suttie, is the acceptance by others of the child's love; that love should not be accepted, even by the parents, as a commonplace to be expected. Appreciation of its love should be made manifest to the child. The parents should evince interest in every little step of the child's progress. One of the greatest thrills a little child experiences comes from its recognition of things, that is its capacity to recognise things by their class names; it will repeat the name of a thing again and again. Parents should show appreciation of this capacity, as well as its capacity for new words. Every little addition to its manners, thoughtfulness, and obedience should be affectionately noticed, especially any spontaneity in its personal relations with strangers. Nothing helps the natural development of the child's nature more than the parent's appreciative interest; and probably nothing quickens the child's intellectual interest so much as this appreciation.

Child psychology, however, would need a series of lectures to itself and not merely the passing remarks I have made. The interest in child psychology for us lies in the fact that to be loved and have its love accepted, and its progress appreciated, are conditions in which the need of a self to realise itself as a whole, gets a chance to move towards satisfaction. There is less chance of inner conflicts when these conditions are fulfilled.

How important the satisfaction of this need is can be seen from the fact that the late Dr. Ian Suttie[1] built his whole theory of Love and Hate upon it. He believed that every breakdown could be traced to the child's reaction to having its love rejected or unresponded to. His appreciation of the Christian religion was based on its capacity to satisfy this need and to dissipate the morbid guilt which haunts so many. To him the relationship of the child to the mother was the most important relationship affecting its whole psychological development. When the child feels insecure in the mother or father's affection it reacts in ways that may lead to deep inferiority feelings, or neurotic illness, or delinquency. On the other hand it may, as it grows older, find a compensation for the loss of mother-love in the social environment.

Like Dr. Suttie, Dr. Karen Horney[2] believes that all breakdown is due to a disturbance of personal relationships. The failure of the child to receive love or to have its own love accepted often leads to what she calls 'a neurotic need for affection'. Here the need to love is overwhelmed by the excessive need to be loved. There is a compulsive seeking for love. Insecurity in our personal relationships gives rise to what Dr. Horney describes as *basic anxiety,* the breeding ground of all neurosis.

Two illustrations will help us here. One is of a very fine woman who never really broke down although she passed through a severe time in late adolescence. Later she devel-

---

[1] 'Origins of Love and Hate,' Chapter 3.
[2] 'New Ways in Psycho-Analysis'; 'The Neurotic Personality of our Time'; 'Our Inner Conflicts.'

oped a strong tendency to detach herself from others, and also severe hostility feelings against which she had to defend herself. So strong was the tendency to detach herself from others that she would walk miles in detour rather than board a bus in which she saw a colleague. She never went into the staff room for morning tea at the break. Naturally the staff could not make head nor tail of her, and a good deal of misunderstanding was caused that did not make things better. She felt that everybody was hostile to her and that everything menaced her.

The origin of the trouble was simple and conscious. As a child of six she had allowed a little boy to kiss her. She felt guilty, so guilty that she went and confessed what she had done to her mother. The latter foolishly told the child's rather tyrannical father, who not only severely reprimanded the child but kept asking her until she was nearly twelve years of age whether she had done such a thing again. The child became afraid to meet her father lest the subject would again he broached. If she spoke to a boy at school, or one or two boys walked a little way with her on the way home from school she felt fearfully guilty and afraid the father would know. She reacted as if she felt: 'If father does not love me it is because I am bad'. That fear of the father's disapproval spread until she became afraid of anyone's disapproval. She lived in fear of disapproval. Alongside of this fear of disapproval grew the hostility. That, I think, came from the fact that the child would feel a certain amount of injustice that the incident was not allowed to pass away; the sense of guilt with its unconscious demand for punishment became so strong that she reached the verge of complete breakdown.

She had a deep and natural interest in religion. There was always the ulterior motive, however, that it might dissipate her guilty feelings. The repeated failure of her religion to do this, and an increasing bias towards social detachment tended to extend her hostility and sense of injustice to God. Envy of other people's happiness began to creep in; jealousy followed as it naturally would, and the hostility feelings grew so strong that defence-symptoms were developed.

At the root of the woman's trouble was the thwarted need for affection. Her detachment was not due to any lack of affection for others, but from the unconscious fear that if she showed affection she would be rebuffed. Personal relations were disturbed and were always insecure. She could develop no spontaneous relations with her superiors even when she was under a chief who was everything that was helpful.

Here is an illustration of an older man. He was sixty-five when his symptoms appeared. He had no energy, had lost interest in things and had frequent spells of depression. He had retired from business at fifty-five. His trouble was one which Suttie's theory explains admirably. His mother had not been a very demonstrative woman although a good mother in other ways. She had been a very busy woman helping her husband to build up a business. As a young man he went to one of the dominions, but only stayed a year. When he came home his father suggested to the elder brother that they had better take him into the business. The brother was not too happy about the suggestion as he was not sure that the business was large enough to keep three going. However, he consented. The relations between the two brothers were always good, and the patient spoke with affection and gratitude of his elder brother. But at the back of the patient's mind there was always the feeling that he could be done without. Probably this was the reason why he retired early. The brother's son came into the business, and the feeling that he could be done without was accentuated.

When he retired he enjoyed doing odd jobs about the house for his wife, and he received a good deal of appreciation, for his family were not all grown up. As the years passed he found that he did not receive the same appreciation; his little jobs were taken for granted. The mother gave more and more attention to the family. He noticed that during the fuel crisis his wife kept telling him to be careful with the coal; when the eldest son came home, however, and emptied the coal scuttle on the fire no deprecating word was said. There were numberless little things he noticed that a healthy mind would not have seen at all. He felt that he was no more the head of the house, that they could all do without him—*that he would not be missed* if he died the next day. All that was repressed and only came to light in the analysis; so, too, did the memory of little illnesses when his mother then gave him great attention. It was this memory that determined his illness, if I am right in applying Dr. Suttie's theory here. He became ill to have the affection and attention he received before he retired and when he first retired. Instead of sympathy and attention, however, from his wife and children he was made to feel that he could easily overcome his symptoms. As the family physician could find nothing organically wrong he was told that his depressed feelings were nothing to worry about. Steadily he grew worse; and subconsciously the feeling that had made him retire from business—that he would not be missed and could be done without—took a grip of his mind and physical symptoms of a hysterical character made their appearance. There was really no ground for the thought that he would not be missed; but the need for affection, the need to be wanted, with its insatiable demands on the affection of his wife and family, were stronger than his perception of the actual situation—indeed, distorted the real situation. His symptoms were the unconscious attempt to get that affection and attention by illness. As Suttie puts it, the mind works on the memory of early experiences and it is as if his mind had said: 'Mother is always kind when one is ill'.

We shall have occasion to return to this theme when dealing with inner conflicts; and we shall now turn to another personality-need.

The Need for Status

2. The second need arising out of the conditions in which personality is realised is *The Need for Status*. Just as the child to be healthy minded needs to feel secure in the parent's affection and to have its own love accepted, so there is a need in the child to feel that it is accepted by the group or community of which it is a part. In other words, we all seek recognition by our group. The old idea that we had a Herd Instinct in virtue of which we felt uncomfortable away from the crowd and had a comfortable feeling in proximity to the crowd was quite inadequate to express all that is implied by the need for social status. It is this need that is the psychological basis of the demand for a 'classless society' as well as of many other social phenomena. It is from this need that there springs the behaviour-tendency or process towards 'socialisation'.

We are not concerned here with sociological implications of this need, but only with its significance for human breakdown. Just as we need and fear the loss of love—probably the deepest fear in a child—so we need the recognition and approval of our group and fear its disapproval. All sense of guilt (in the true meaning of that much abused term) is generated by the fear of losing our status in our group or the fear of losing our status with God. The patient I mentioned whose neurosis first appeared in the uncomfortable feelings experienced in the Masonic Meeting was suffering from the fear of losing his status among his fellow-masons. Adler believed that every neurosis began in inferiority-feelings, and his compensating 'will to power' was simply the manner in which the individual chose to assert or to gain his status in spite of his feelings of inferiority. Dr. Karen Horney lists amongst her 'neurotic character-trends' the need for approval,[1] two of the characteristics of which are 'an indiscriminate need to please others', and an 'automatic living up to the expectations of others'. Why the indiscriminate need to please others or the automatic living up to the expectations of others if it is not to keep our status with those we are trying to please or whose expectations we are trying to live up to? The group whose approval we seek, or whose expectations we try to live up to may be a very small group, no more than our own family and friends, or it may be a larger group such as our church or the members of our own profession. At the root of many professional men's neurosis this need to keep the status of their vocation is very strong, and but for it they might not have broken down. This applies especially to the clergy, lawyers, and doctors. The loss of professional status is often the dreaded thing. To lose status is to lose the respect of others, and indeed our self-respect. Was it not the loss of status that was deplored as one of the worst effects of unemployment?

Both positively and negatively this need works upon us. In virtue of it we tend to accept uncritically our cultural and social standards and we become afraid to violate them.

---

[1] 'Self-Analysis,' p. 54 f.

We cannot afford to be the odd man out. On the negative side this need for status tends to make us repress any behaviour-tendencies that would endanger our status. It is at the root of a great deal of repression. Any departure from the normal standards or social conventions has to be *rationalised,* or it must be repressed. Nudism is a good example of rationalisation of an exhibitionist tendency which in most people is integrated and controlled spontaneously. Even in perfectly normal people the overlooking of their status can arouse a good deal of resentment. Let a Mayor be overlooked when the invitations are sent out for some official function and . . .! Fortunately most people are not conscious of the need of status until it is threatened or overlooked. When it is threatened by some behaviour-tendency whose expression would cause a loss of moral prestige, it is more than likely to be repressed. What other people think of us has a far greater influence on our motives of behaviour than we are willing to allow.

To gain status is often the motive behind achievement. It is not a good motive because when the status is gained it is found to be anything but satisfying. A great deal of social climbing has status for its end.

Its main interest to us here is that it is the fear of losing status in the eyes of others or in our own eyes that causes us to repress behaviour-tendencies that are not socially approved. Some people cannot believe that they can think and even conceive in phantasy certain kinds of behaviour until it is forced on them by their dreams. Others, again, will be found who worry about what people would think if they knew that they had done this or thought that.

I remember two patients whose main symptoms were centred round a compulsive tendency to read books in which they had no real interest. But they dare not leave them unread. The motive of the compulsion was that they could not bear the idea of anyone in their group having read a book that they had not. Naturally there was no intellectual gain from their compulsive reading.

This need for status is closely connected with the religious sense of guilt. Think of the part played in religious experience by the fear of losing status with God. St. Paul's theology of Justification is simply the attempt to show how while we are yet sinners we have status before God. The morbid sense of religious guilt is generated by this fear of losing, not the love of God, but status before Him. And for many an Evangelical the greatness of Christ is that through His death He restored that status to us. Fortunately for me, the psychologist is not called upon to validate or invalidate a theology of Justification or Atonement. There can be no question, however, but that such theology is closely connected with the generation of the sense of guilt and also with its removal.

Need for Rational Unity

3. We come now to a Need that is very closely allied with the fundamental need to realise our personality as a whole. *That is the Need for Moral and Rational Unity.* The self cannot but attempt to unify all its experience. Here the mind becomes the organ of personality, as Field Marshal Smuts[1] has pointed out. The dynamic principle underlying this need is Reason. We must be careful to differentiate this principle from the capacity to reason things out, or to reflect upon our experiences. This latter is but one of its manifestations; and it is more accurately termed *intelligence*. We are thinking of the urge to reflection rather than the processes of reflection. That urge or need is Reason—

[1] 'Holism and Evolution,' Chapter 9.

the dynamic tendency to synthesise our experiences and our knowledge. Reason, I believe with Hobhouse, is a dynamic tendency of the self towards an all-embracing harmony. 'It is the impulse, not merely to interpret experience that men have actually accumulated, but to extend the synthesis to all possible experiences. It is the organising principle of thought!'[1]

I believe, further, that it is the organising principle of conscience. Our moral experience must be harmonised, as well as our intellectual experience. No thinker can live comfortably with a contradiction; and certainly no one can live at peace with a moral contradiction. There is a drive for truth, and there is a drive for moral harmony.

This is the psychological explanation of the need for a philosophy of life which is being so much emphasised by schools of therapy other than psycho-analysts.[2] It is the content of the philosophy of life that gives content as well as direction to the will. It gives rational standards to conscience. Jung goes so far as to state: 'A psycho-neurosis must be understood as the suffering of a human being who has not discovered what life means to him'.[3] He states the same thing in religious terms when he says that a neurosis arises from the lack of that which religion gives to all its children.

It was the curse of a great deal of psychology from Hume to McDougall that it subordinated Reason to appetite and the passions. According to this type of psychology the function of reason was to find the means for satisfying the passions. In Freud all the ends of the Ego are set by the Id,

---

[1] 'The Rational Good,' p. 94. Hobhouse. (London: George Allen & Unwin Ltd.)
[2] Cf. 'An Introduction to Psychological Medicine,' Gordon, Harris and Rees. Chapter 4.
[3] 'Modern Man in Search of a Soul.' Jung, p. 260.

and reason is made synonymous with intellectual judgment, and is the property of the Reality-Ego. McDougall contended that the reason could set no ends. Here I am contending that Reason is a property of the self, and is indeed the principle whereby it works to realise itself as a harmonious whole. Intellect we have in common with the animal and no doubt a good deal of our intellectual activity is determined by the necessity of satisfying biological needs. The higher ends, however, the ends which differentiate man from the animals are set by Reason; they are related to personality-needs. Intellect must not be confused with Reason; the latter is the principle of harmony, the dynamic endeavour to achieve rational unity in our experience of the external world, and harmony within our inner life. It is not irrelevant to mention that patients with compulsions, anxiety-states, and fears worry not only about their compulsions, anxiety, or fears but also about the fact that these are irrational. A woman suffering from the fear of going out alone, worries as much about the irrationality of it as she does about the fact that she cannot go out. A man worries because he has a fear that he will collapse in the street; he knows as well as I do that there are no objective grounds for his fear. Such patients get the fear of insanity. A woman gives a charwoman a tin of meat and then worries lest the food is contaminated and that if the woman eats it she will die. She knows the whole thing is irrational, but instead of that dispersing her fear, it adds the fear that she will go mad. The fear is generated by the fact that the mind cannot harmonise objective facts with its feelings. Reason is thwarted; the drive for harmony of experience with feeling is blocked. Consciousness, as Collingwood says, is corrupted.[1]

---

[1] 'Principles of Art,' p. 40.

At the moment we are concerned not with the thwarting of Reason but with its positive function of seeking rational unity. The self cannot but seek to synthesise its life; it is involved in all its experiences, and must seek meaning to them as well as its own status amongst these experiences. It is not only conscious but self-conscious. It knows that it knows, and it knows its ignorance. It is conscious of transcending its experience, and hence wants to find meaning in its experience.

I must be careful not to fall into philosophy while emphasising that the need for rational unity compels the self to seek for some meaning in its experience of life. From the psychological point of view this need for a philosophy of life[1] (which may be expressed in one's religious beliefs or faith) is a purely functional necessity and has nothing to do with any particular philosophy or religion. Indeed it is the creator of every religion, and every philosophy. Until the individual has found some moral standards which flow from his meaning of life he is rudderless; and if he is seriously minded at all he will be conscious of psychological and moral conflicts. The lack of a philosophy of life is always a sign of immaturity, for no man can be said to be adjusted to life unless he has come to terms with what the late Principal Cairns called *The Riddle of the World*.

We shall have more to say about this religious need later. For it is a need and not merely a functional necessity. We cannot, however, leave this fundamental need for rational unity until we see its relevance to our moral life. On its moral side the organ of this need is *Conscience*. In our next lecture we shall have to deal with the guilt which conscience

---

[1] See 'Character and Nervous Disorders' (McKenzie), p. 30 ff. Also Cf. 'Psychology for Ministers and Social Workers' (Guntripp), p. 103 f.

can generate, and which is such a characteristic symptom of so much neurotic illness. 'Every neurotic suffers from a bad conscience',[1] wrote one very skilled psychotherapist, and certainly there are few patients who do not bring some evidence of being conscience-stricken. From the point of view of conscience we see Reason as working towards inner moral harmony; it makes it difficult for us to live with moral contradictions in our lives. Conscience itself, we may define as *the dynamic tendency of the self to co-ordinate and regulate its behaviour according to ethical, religious, and cultural standards consciously or unconsciously accepted*. It has both negative and positive functions. Conscience does not legislate, but it judges according to our knowledge of good and evil, and its judgments are accompanied by some of our deepest emotions. Amongst man's noblest feelings are those experienced by him when in defiance of society he has stood firm by some judgment of his conscience. To say that a man is ruled by principle is to say that he is ruled by his conscience. To speak of a man's integrity in public or business life is to say that his actions are motivated by his conscience. There is nothing rigid about a healthy conscience, because it is always accessible to reason whose servant it is. Of the strength of its negative feelings we have all some experience: remorse, regret, shame, humiliation and self-condemnation. In neurotics these emotions can reach an intense degree. Most moralists acknowledge its authority; but its power can be tremendous in its effects upon the individual soul. Some of the worst types of human breakdown are due to the repression of a conscience that was once alive.

Let me give two illustrations. The first is of a man suffering from the fear that he could not hold his job; he was

---

[1] 'Anxiety Conditions and their Cure,' by Stekel, p. 22.

depressed, and suffered a good deal from sleeplessness. He had been discharged from the army on account of neurotic symptoms. He had been brought up in a religious home, and had himself been a church worker. He was married to a really capable and understanding wife. His dreams led back to a long history of sexual promiscuity dating from almost the first years of married life. The promiscuous habit had become so strong that when he was recovering his mind began to play with the promiscuous ideas again, and phantasy was almost obsessive. The man's conscience simply refused to live with a moral contradiction.

The second is that of a commercial traveller. He was recovering from an anxiety-state when one day he became very depressed and fear stricken. One of his dreams showed that he had had an opportunity of making a good deal on the black market, and apparently he had played with the idea and repressed it. Before he could indulge himself his conscience and the fear of being found out broke him.[1]

Here we can pay tribute to the work done by the psychoanalysts on the development of consience, or as they call it 'the super ego'.[1] It is to them we owe most of what we know about the strength of the prohibitions the conscience can exercise; and they have done the pioneering work on the development of conscience. As we shall be considering this in our next lecture it is enough at the moment to be reminded that the authority of conscience cannot be ignored or undermined if we are to understand and remedy neurotic breakdown. Lesser followers of Freud have often attempted to do this with their patients, with disastrous results. Doctors or psychotherapists who do this are still labouring under the false idea that expression of appetite or desire is

---

[1] Cf. 'Modern Man in Search of a Soul,' p. 223.
[2] Freud: 'Ego and the Id,' 'Man, Morals and Society,' Flügel.

the cure of repression of appetite or desire; whereas the cure lies in bringing the repressed behaviour-tendencies into harmony with the natural drive of conscience for moral unity. The conscience is not a socially created entity however much the standards by which it attempts to co-ordinate and regulate behaviour-tendencies are derived from our social environment; it is of the very nature of personality. The moral problem cannot be ignored. To lift the inhibitions from repressed behaviour-tendencies without putting some kind of moral control in their place is to undermine personality, to say nothing of the fact that to persuade a patient to defy his prohibitions may land the patient in an asylum! The psychotherapist who does not respect the conscience or does not understand its nature is a public danger.

The Organising Activity of the Mind

No account of human nature could be complete without some reference to the spontaneous manner in which the mind organises its conations, its feelings and its thought. Order in the inner life is as characteristic as order in the phenomena of the external world. From early infancy the mind synthesises the impressions from the external world into percepts; the percepts become synthesised into concepts.

From the point of view of needs the same kind of organising activity can be observed. Our needs organise our emotions, direct our conations and elicit thought or ideas at every stage of life. The infant's first interests are all directed by its need for nutrition, cleanliness, and care. Psycho-analysts have made a great deal of this early period in the child's life and have even used the developing interests of the child to denote types of character in the adult. There is the *oral* stage in the infant's life when the child's main activity and interest is in food. Then there is the period when in the interest of cleanliness the mother directs the interests of the child towards its excretory activities; this is called the *anal* stage. Finally the child spontaneously directs its interest towards its body, especially its sex organs. This is called the *genital* stage. There can be no doubt that the difficulties and pleasure the child encounters at these stages of life leave impressions which affect behaviour-tendencies; but it is very doubtful if they are such as to justify us in speaking of an *Oral* character, or an *Anal* character, or a *Genital* character in the adult. Nor is there any doubt that psychological effects of that period can often be observed in adult neurotics, and that some perversions have their origin here. I remember a woman who had the compulsive tendency to suck at her dental plates until her mouth was sore. For some reason there was a regression to the sucking stage; and in people, apparently free from neurotic tendencies, to see, handle and kiss a woman's breasts gives intense pleasure. Anal interests and even perversions are not uncommon; and pre-occupation with the body is often found especially at adolescence. It is doubtful, however, whether these childish left-overs can determine character, although they may account for character-trends. *Character can only be predicated of a self.*[1] In any case the tracing of one of these behaviour-trends or left-overs does not cure it. What has happened is that the self has failed to organise its interests into one or other of what we shall characterise in a moment as sentiments. For example, anal or excretory interests are normally organised into what is regarded as the sentiment of cleanliness in a well-brought-up child. *A sentiment is the organisation of impulse, ideas and emotions round the idea of some object.*

[1] Cf. Ward's 'Psychological Principles', Chapter 18.

The capacity of the self to organise into sentiments the behaviour-tendencies connected with biological and personality-needs is the most important phenomenon we have to take note of here.

We have already seen that biological needs become personal ends. As a consequence they must be organised within our moral sentiments, otherwise the self will be dominated by them. They must be integrated with moral ideals. No man is safe until the sex tendencies are controlled by a moral self. A sex ethic is essential in any moral life. Classical ethics emphasised this when it included *temperance* as one of the cardinal virtues, its opposite, *lust* being included in the Church's catalogue of cardinal sins. Courage has always been looked upon as a virtue, but it is only possible when the tendencies associated with the need to preserve the organism are organised within the moral sentiments. *Gluttony* as we have seen is included in the list of cardinal sins, showing that even the appetite of hunger has to be moralised.

We are more concerned, however, with the personality-needs and the behaviour-tendencies associated with them. The need to love and to be loved soon manifests itself in the child's life. Quite spontaneously the child's love-interests organise themselves round the idea of the mother and father and the other members of the household. He needs their love and approval in order that his personal relations with them may be harmonious, and he wants to love them. Without their love and the acceptance of his love, the child has no sense of security. This sentiment of love for the members of the household begins spontaneously to control his behaviour-tendencies, and even his behaviour-mechanisms, both positively and negatively. Positively the sentiment will direct his tendencies so as to please mother, or gain the approval of father; and he will just as spontaneously inhibit tendencies of which they might disapprove. If the sentiments for the members of the household are growing spontaneously, the child inevitably tends to conform to the standards of the household both in his thought and behaviour. What *he wants to do* and what they *think he ought to do* tend to coincide. Thus there is no conflict between his wants and the wanted objects in which the former are satisfied. Naturally such an ideal state does not often occur, and there is often a conflict between what he wants and what the household approve. We shall see the result of such a conflict later, for the child tends to internalise the standards of behaviour set by the household, and, unless these internalised standards are assimilated, they stand over against the child's behaviour-tendencies as restraints against which he may be inwardly fighting. Along with the sentiments for the members of the household other interests are rapidly forming—interest in natural phenomena, in the life around him in the streets or countryside. The mind of the child quickly begins to get order into all these different objects in the form of percepts and class-names. The appreciation of the parents here, as we have seen, deepens and strengthens the child's interest in knowledge, and may be a deciding factor in the direction the child's intellectual interest takes.

Later the growing boy or girl acquires abstract sentiments which are closely connected with those complex tendencies we know as sympathy, gratitude, unselfishness, and reverence as well. Truth comes to be loved for its own sake; likewise justice, freedom, love, motherhood, goodness and beauty. These abstract sentiments grow step by step with the concrete sentiments. Spontaneously, then, interests, behaviour-tendencies, emotions and ideas become organised within sentiments and become spontaneously controlled,

If, as we have contended, the vital thing in personal life is not the *wants* but the *wanted objects,* then this natural tendency to sentiment-making is one of the most important activities of the self. Growing with all these sentiments is the sentiment of self-regard[1] and respect for others. It is the sentiment which educationists should keep well in mind. Unless the idea of the self is healthy, the capacity of the self to canalise its energies along the line of self-imposed ends is likely to be weak. The Will does not get a chance to develop. Although sentiments are not character they give the objects through which character expresses itself.

It is in this sentiment-making we must look for the secret of what James called 'the once-born'. Apparently the absence of the debilitating conflicts of the neurotic and the moral conflicts of the 'converted' in these *once-born* is due to the fact that their interests and sentiments were early in life organised round objects which there was no need to repudiate in later life. Their 'wanted objects' were consistent not only with their 'wants' but with the demands of their conscience. Their conscience was not occupied in prohibitions or compulsions, and was thus left free to guide the behaviour-tendencies. Their moral sentiments controlled spontaneously their behaviour-tendencies without the need for coercion.

There is no limit to the number of objects round the idea of which the mind can organise its emotions, conations and ideas, in other words there is no limit to the number of sentiments an individual can acquire. They may range from the leisure interests in football or bridge to the æsthetic sentiment for beauty; the moral sentiments for justice, freedom, and the personal virtues, the political sentiments for

---

[1] McDougall contended this was the most important sentiment. See Introduction to 'Social Psychology' and 'Outline'.

democracy, fascism, communism, or monarchy; the intellectual sentiment for truth; the vocational sentiment for our profession, and the highest sentiment of all, the religious.

For the psychotherapist the interest of sentiments lies in the fact that he has a hard job to lead back to health and happiness those individuals who have no background of sentiments of a really comprehensive kind. If he has to re-educate a person he can only do it by helping him to acquire sentiments that can really organise his life as a whole. To have no sentiments is to lack spiritual resources, and that may mean boredom and discontent, or a pre-occupation with sex or bodily ailments. Not a little of sex interest is an escape from a life that has no deep interests or sentiments.

Very often this lack of permanent interests shows itself in men who have retired from business; it may show itself in women who have given no thought to anything outside their husband and children. When the children have grown up these women simply don't know what to do with themselves, and can become the prey of depression, anxieties and worry. With the children outside the need for care, life has lost its meaning for them and they crack.

We are now within some distance of an answer to Professor Hocking's question: What is original human nature? What do we start with on our task of realising our personality as a whole? How do we turn potentially human nature into actual human nature—adult, stable, mature and capable of co-operating with its fellows and entering into those personal relationships in which happiness is a reality? Without a knowledge of human nature, of the needs of personality and of their associated behaviour-tendencies, human breakdown just bewilders, as does a great deal of human behaviour. When we know that a child is stealing money from the mother's purse to give away to school fellows because he is not sure of his status with them, and is taking this way of gaining a sense of security with them, we are really on the way to curing the child of his delinquency. When we know that it is the natural spontaneous tendency of the child to acquire sentiments which organise his behaviour-tendencies and to fill his life with interests, then we know that we have allies within the child which will reinforce our attempts to help him to realise his personality as a whole. When we know that the child begins life with a capacity to canalise his energy, direct his emotions, and control his thoughts along the line of self-imposed ends we are strengthened in our endeavours to guide his wants towards 'wanted objects' that will not conflict with the ends of personality. When we grasp the idea of the prospective aim of personality we are less likely to attempt to make the child what God never intended it to be. *The image of God is simply this drive in us all towards completeness.* Not one of our needs will then be despised; all will be made to subserve the ends of personality, and in the degree they do, life and personality are being realised, and the image of God is expressing itself.

Summary

Here, as far as it is possible within the limits of these lectures, is our account of original human nature. It begins with certain specific needs in the interests of which we acquire behaviour-tendencies by which we satisfy these needs.These needs are not separate instincts independent of the organism and the personality as a whole. They find their meaning in the organism and personality which they subserve. In man these become personal ends and not simply something that belongs to the 'flesh'. In virtue of

man's capacity to perceive relations, he can subordinate
both the needs and behaviour-tendencies to his own selfish
pleasure or ends. Immediately he does so there is set up
either a conflict which may result in neurosis or a condition
in which the possibility of realising a personality at all is
undermined.

Man's needs are not exhausted in a catalogue of his biological impulses or ends. He is a self with an individuality
of his own. The very nature of that self is to realise his
personality as a whole. That is done in a social environment in which the most important factors are personal
relationships, and also in the society of which he is a member. To realise himself as a whole and to become adjusted
to society he needs love and to be capable of giving love,
for that is the bond of personal relationships, and indeed
is the bond that binds him to his country with its cultural
traditions and its Common Good, in which he realises his
individual ends or goods. There is the need for status, the
need to be accepted as a member of the society in which
his personal relationships should be spontaneous. Still more
profound is that need for rational and moral unity in his
life. In satisfying this need the cultural, political, social,
and moral as well as the religious traditions of the community are created. These become the first content of the
individual mind, and they provide his moral standards of
conscience; they provide him with his knowledge of good
and evil, and according to that knowledge his conscience
co-ordinates and regulates his behaviour-tendencies.

The growth of human nature or personality is not just the
outcome of the interplay between needs and social environment. The self is an active agent, indeed *the* active agent.
To the degree the individual organises his behaviour-
tendencies within sentiments, they become directed by the

interests of ends vitally related to personality. Sex behaviour-tendencies, emotions, ideas, become organised within the sentiment of love and are thus regulated by the loved object. Until the individual has organised his sex tendencies within his moral sentiments or within the sentiment for a member of the other sex he cannot feel secure in his love life. His need for rational unity gets full play in his intellectual life, while his need for moral unity offers an opportunity for all sorts of social interests and moral endeavour. There is no end to the sentiments he may acquire, which is another way of saying that there is no limit to the whole towards which the self can advance.

OUR INNER CONFLICTS AND CHARACTER-STRUCTURES

WE have now seen what kind of answer must be given to Professor Hocking's question: 'What is original Human Nature?' Human nature is no mere passive thing to be shaped by environmental pressures. Implicit in human nature from the beginning is an ideal, a 'telos'—what philosophers call a 'nisus'—a formative effort towards an end. The end itself is the realisation of the self-conscious, independent individual experiencing himself as a harmonious whole.

The soil in which the seed grows is the social environment. Both the seed and the soil are dynamic. The personal environment, the cultural standards, the social, moral and religious traditions act upon us dynamically in the sense that they condition us. They cannot create human personality. Original human nature, the seed with its 'telos', is also dynamic and may resist and even change the traditions which play such an important part in its development as a realised whole.

That is one of the most vital differences between man and the lower animals. The animal can only modify itself, not its environment; man can do both. He can modify his behaviour-tendencies or change his environment. He cannot 'change human nature' in the sense that he can substitute something else for the biological and personality-needs; nor can he make his end anything less than the self-conscious whole without becoming less than a man. Herbart asked: 'Does the human being bring with him into the world his future shape or does he not?' We can answer 'Yes' if he means: Does man bring with him into the world a 'telos', an implicit end? But if he means: Is it pre-determined that man will realise his 'telos' or end? The answer must be in the negative. Given normal conditions 'the plant will not miss its end, nor the bird newly hatched fail to fly'; but there are no conditions known to us in which we can guarantee that the child will realise its implicit end. Some individuals, with apparently the best conditions of environmental pressures, fail tragically; others have achieved personality and character in spite of severe hostile conditions. Man has *to achieve* his personality and character. The realised whole is never a spontaneous development. The individual is always the chief agent of his own destiny. Personality grows in conflict with its conditions not in virtue of them. A growing adolescent may have a hard fight to win his own individuation in virtue of being brought up in 'a good home' while another achieves his in spite of 'a bad home'. It is one of the commonplaces of psychotherapy that the great majority who come seeking the psychotherapist's help come from 'good homes'. 'Good homes' are not seldom the breeding centres of neurosis. We have the psychological paradox that the more lax the home is in moral standards the less likelihood there is of a nervous breakdown or of neurotic conflict.

Freedom from neurotic conflict, however, is not necessarily a mark of achieved personality; indeed it is as often as not the sign of the lack of personality and character. That can be seen in the often noted observation that the psychotherapist gets few Roman Catholic patients. No one would suggest that Roman Catholics are marked by a greater degree of ethical maturity. On the contrary, it might be that easy absolution, the religious sanction of paying their moral debts by a system of penance preserves them from what the Americans call 'a guilt block', but does not inspire them towards a more adult ethical ideal. There are individuals who have no conscious moral ideals, and do not want them; they have no direction to their lives except biological needs. 'The natural man has only two primal passions, to get and to beget—to get the means of sustenance (and today a little more) and to beget his kind. Satisfy these, and he looks neither before nor after, but goeth forth to his work and to his labour until the evening and returning sweats in oblivion without a thought of whence or whither'.[1] The personality-needs may have been swamped by external conditions or may have never been stimulated into consciousness or ignored in the pursuit of the pleasure which the satisfaction of biological needs can offer.

That I may be understood in my reference to 'good homes' as the breeding place of neurosis, let me give you an illustration: A.B.[2] had a serious breakdown not long after he left college and started teaching. For fifteen years he did no work. There was a strong negativism and a refusal to eat, and there was one long period when the patient lay with his face to the wall. The parents were as good and saintly people as I ever expect to meet. Nevertheless, at the worst periods of the severe neurosis of their son, the parents were the objects of hostile feelings and of language almost unprintable. The real root of the trouble was the fight of the lad to win his own individuation. He had a neurotic need for their affection. That character-structure made him shrink in fear from anything his parents were likely to disapprove of. He could not *bear* their disapproval. It was not

---

[1] Sir William Osler: 'Ingersoll Lecture on Immortality', pp. 20—21.
[2] Cf. 'Man, Morals and Society,' by Flügel, p. 87.

E

that he *feared* their disapproval so much as that he could not *bear* it. The strong drive to win his own individuation, to express his own individuality and not be a mere echo of his parents and the home atmosphere, came up against the contradictory neurotic need for their affection, with its tendency to shrink from any thought or act of which he thought they were likely to disapprove. The conflict between the two structures broke him down. Even today, when he is back teaching and his affection and relationship to his parents are of the adult pattern, there is still a tendency to shrink from any expression of himself not in accordance with their ideas. He could not bear to hurt them, and certainly would not argue with them.

It is this drive to win one's own individuation that is behind the desire of many adolescents of both sexes to leave home. Hence we must be careful to see that our 'good homes' leave the young free to express their own individuality, and not compel them either to rebel or to acquire a strong tendency to restrict their lives within too narrow limits or prevent them from acquiring a positive conscience that can become their guide and not their policeman. 'Good' parents are often more afraid that their children will go wrong than desirous of actively guiding them to love the good; such parents almost invariably make it hard for the young to realise their personality without severe conflicts.

Given our original human nature and the personal and social environment in which personality can be realised, it is even then almost impossible to grow to maturity without psychological and moral conflict. That very objective psychological observer, the late Dr. Rivers, noted the fact that 'Childhood is one long conflict between individual instinctive tendencies and the social traditions and ideals of society. Whether the outcome of this conflict will be a genius or a paranoiac, a criminal or a philanthropist, a good citizen or a wastrel, depends, in some measure, we do not yet know with any degree of exactness, in what measure, on education, on the direction which is given by the environment, material, psychological and social, to the energy engendered in the conflicts made necessary by the highly complex character of the past of our race'.[1] I should not myself put it exactly in that way today. The assumption of Rivers is that the environment is the vital thing; whereas I should say that the reaction of the individual is the deciding factor. Be that as it may, he is undoubtedly right in recognising the fact that childhood and adolescence is one long conflict between the seed and the soil, between the 'telos' and the conditions in which that 'telos' reaches completeness. The self may have contradictory structures, as we saw in the case I have cited. We may take false ways to realise our needs, both biological and personal. Our sentiments may conflict and our conscience may remain merely prohibitive, and thus compel us to acquire character-structures which tend to limit our lives within very narrow limits, or to accept a perfectionist standard below which we dare not fall. These conflicts are not necessarily between libidinous desires and what is allowed by social standards; nor need they be between our 'will to power' and the wills of other people. No doubt there are individuals who break down to get their own way and then rule the roost from their beds; or whose sexual desires are more than moral reality can allow; but there is no necessary debilitating conflict between our biological needs and our personality needs. Such conflicts, I believe, are always the outcome of a wrong and narrow conception of the ethical status of the organism[2]

---

[1] 'Instinct and The Unconscious,' p. 157.
[2] Cf. Brünner's 'Christianity and Civilisation', p. 96.

and its biological needs, or of some early experience which gave the behaviour-tendencies a perverted twist, such as homosexuality, or which led to repression. Such repressed early experiences create a complex which may affect our thought, emotions and behaviour, and lead to psycho-neurotic trouble.

Complex and Character-Structure

That brings me to a point I did not make too clear in my last Tate Lectures. A kindly reviewer wrote me a personal letter in which he said: 'There are one or two points I would have liked to discuss with you. I had a feeling that you had gone over almost exclusively from complex-analysis to character-analysis. I recognise the tremendously important advance of people like Suttie, Horney and Fromm from the biological Freudian point of view, to a more sociological approach. . . . But in clinical work I find myself having to move back and forth between complex-analysis and character-analysis. I find discussion of a character-trait so often brings up a chunk of early memories and a crop of dreams which clearly have their roots in some fairly well defined age level of childhood. Again, the analysis of a complex forces a character-trait to the front. But I expect you would agree. There is not room in four lectures to say everything.'

My friend, if he reads these lectures, will find that I have gone from character-analysis to the main-spring of the self for the ultimate reason for human breakdown! I find that the ultimate cause of the kind of personality-failure which leads to nervous disorders and maladjustments lies in the inability of the self to canalise its energy, thought and emotions along the line of self chosen ends, or its inability to integrate its childhood experience with more mature experience. Conscience, behaviour-tendencies, emotions and reason are not unified; experience is out of harmony with feeling.

When one has stated the ultimate cause, however, one has still to seek the immediate causes for the self's inability to integrate, and thus early experiences must be explored to which the character-structures may be reaction-formations. Almost all the perversions and not a few of the phobias have their origins in the experiences of childhood. You will remember that, when I was defining the ultimate causes of breakdown, I was careful to add to the inability of the self to canalise its energy its inability to integrate its early experiences. That helps us to differentiate the complex from the character-structure. A complex is created by some experience which the self had to repress for some reason or another, and was thus unable to integrate it with the rest of experience.

An illustration will help us here. J.C. was a young woman who had broken off her engagement. She complained that when she was with her beloved she became anxious and almost panic-stricken. She also experienced the same feelings in church, especially at the evening service. She loved the church and had done a great deal of work in connection with it, and the fact that she was unable to enjoy the services when she went, distressed her greatly. I cannot recall any distortion in her character at all. Apart from these symptoms she seemed a very well-balanced individual. The whole thing cleared up suddenly with the remembrance of a dream and its associations. The dream was that she was passing through a churchyard, and on top of a gravestone she saw two pennies lying. She felt afraid and woke up. The dream immediately brought back the memory, which had been thoroughly repressed. When she was in her teens she went out with the farm-servant boy to bring in the cows for milking. When the two were in the cowshed the boy tried to assault her. She resisted successfully. The boy, now afraid she would tell her father, the farmer, offered her two pence not to tell what he had done. Now, the love-making of her fiance must have tended to arouse memories of this incident, which were firmly repressed, and the guilt and fear attached to the incident filled her conscious mind. In other words, she got the emotions without the memory of the incident; emotions were disassociated from the memory. Hence the unaccountable feelings when with her lover. The evangelical preaching of the Sunday evenings in her Methodist Church must have also tended to arouse the emotions without the attached memory. Hence the guilt feelings. She could not recall encouraging the approaches of the boy, but she remembered that she thought her father and mother would blame her. The recovery of the dissociated memory and its integration with her adult experience and attitude to things which happen in childhood and early adolescence completely freed her from her fears.

It is my opinion that a complex is always the outcome of some early experience that has either been repressed or was experienced at an age when no ideas could associate with the experience. The latter is simply an emotional and conational experience, but without ideas to give it real meaning, and is the more difficult to cure. Hostility feelings are often aroused early in life, and may leave an unaccountable fear that the individual will hurt someone. A child separated from the home at an early age—e.g., six to eight months— may have an unbearable sense of insecurity if later in life the parents go on holiday. It is seldom if ever that these very early experiences can be recalled, and even when they have been noted by others and related to the grown-up with the complex, that does not evaporate the symptoms. It always alleviates them if the patient can see conceptually an association between the symptoms and the related experiences.

Sometimes a character-structure will be developed whose main purpose is to help the individual to avoid the feared situation. We shall see later how these structures are formed. Meantime it is enough to note that the value of the analysis of childhood's experiences lies in the fact that it helps us to understand how a complex or character-structure comes to be formed. The analysis does not of itself modify a character-structure; once the character-structure is made conscious to the individual he has then to do something about it. Fears which have their roots in an experience that was repressed may clear up suddenly as in the case related, if the memory is recalled.

Character-structures, in my opinion, are formed as a reaction-formation to a situation as a whole; one needs to know the whole situation in which the individual grew up to be able to explain it thoroughly. On the other hand, some character-structures have grown up in the attempt to satisfy behaviour-tendencies connected with biological or person-ality-needs; sometimes as defences against the strength of behaviour-tendencies. Lying may be the outcome of the neurotic fear of disapproval, as prudery is certainly a defence reaction to its very opposite in the unconscious. We shall find, I think, that distorted structures are attempts at adaptation to social pressures, and that most of our neurotic character-structures are connected in one way or another with our fundamental needs.

It is not uncommon to find in the neurotic individual, and sometimes in the 'normal' individual, character-struc-tures which are incompatible and which lead to contradictory goals. A not uncommon example of this is found in the individual who does not face up to his limitations. One such failed to take a degree through no fault of his own. Instead of facing the fact that he was envious of the men with degrees he simply built up an inflated image of himself, and of his abilities, and then unconsciously demanded that everyone should evaluate him by this inflated image of his own ability. Naturally no one did, and he turned awkward towards those in authority over him. He was at the same time ambitious and, in spite of his inflated image, he had natural ability. His awkwardness then prevented him realising his ambitions and he lived with a continual grudge against his superiors. If his envy of a degree had stirred emulation he could have worked for an external degree and got the chance of openings open only to graduates. Instead, as I have said, he built up the inflated image.

My own conclusions in regard to character-structure formations is that they are the outcome of legitimate needs being thwarted, and the morbid structure is the attempt on the part of the self to restore the balance and to give a sense of security against, either the social situation in which the needs are denied their satisfaction, or inner behaviour-tendencies which the social situation demands to be repressed.

We turn now and see how the formation of character-structures takes place in response to some situation as a whole.

These character-structures have been best described by Dr. Horney and Dr. Erich Fromm. What I want to do is to link the formation of these structures with the thwarted needs to which they are a response. One of the best described structures is the neurotic need for affection.[1] Dr.

---

[1] 'The Neurotic Personality of our Time,' Chapters 6 and 7. See also 'Self-Analysis,' Chapter 2.

Horney tells us that it is manifested in a fear of disapproval, an attempt to live up to the wishes of other people, especially of those whose affection or approval is desired, and often a fear of being alone. Suppose a child for some reason is really deprived of the mother's affection, or the manifestation of that affection; or suppose the child misconceives the mother's attention to a new baby as a withdrawal of her affection from itself. Or the mother may die and the father marry again and the child is sent to live with relatives. Any of these conditions can create what Dr. Suttie called 'separation anxiety'. The child deprived of the conditions which call out the response of its love, may acquire the compulsory tendency to seek affection, and the neurotic need becomes rooted. If it is a new baby, misconceived as a rival for the mother's affection, the child is likely to have hostile feelings both towards the new baby and also towards the mother for the attention which she gives to the usurper. These hostile feelings have to be repressed. The child now feels insecure in its relationship to the mother and the new baby. The child may react by trying to be 'extra good' and obedient under the mask of affection. It will attempt to avoid the appearance of doing anything which would arouse the displeasure of the mother; any displeasure shown by the parent is responded to by a flood of tears out of all proportion to any rebuke which may be passed upon the child. It will fear any separation from the parent, such as going to a boarding school; and it will seek the attention of the mother in all sorts of ways even to the extent of repeated illness which later may develop into invalidism. Should such an individual have the courage to get married, the need for security in the love relationship may get transferred to the partner. There will be insatiable demands upon his or her affection and attention, often accompanied by violent upsets; these may lead to reconciliations which give the neurotic individual a temporary sense of security in the partner's affection. The need for this sense of security in the partner's affection is so strong that it inhibits the natural tendency to love in return. The exhausting demands are now in full swing; and the unconscious hostility to the parents may now be transferred to the partner, making things more difficult still. Envy of the partner's normality leads to jealousy of all his or her interests which are not directly related to the neurotic individual; sexual jealousy is a feature much more marked in some than in others. Towards the partner's friends there will be a compulsive tendency to be 'nice' but also a hypersensitivity to any supposed neglect.

In the above description I am drawing directly from my experiences of these victims of the neurotic need for affection, of which I could instance many cases.

On the other hand, the child, instead of manifesting its need for affection in the above ways, may develop what Dr. Horney calls 'a neurotic need for self-sufficiency and independence'. It is as if the child said: 'Well, if you don't love me, I can do without you'. All through life that individual will avoid any tie which might give him or her the feeling of being dependent on anyone else. The only way of being secure from again being rebuffed is to keep one's distance from others, to keep oneself to oneself. If such a one does marry, the independent attitude will be maintained towards the partner and any children of the marriage. Any demonstration of affection will be treated with scorn or ridicule, although in other respects the behaviour will be considerate and correct. There will be no pampering, no demonstration that might give the idea of dependence. Socially such a person may keep his personal relationships intact, but there will be no deep intimacies.

The more extreme reaction to the thwarted need for affection may express itself in extreme detachment as in the case of the woman who would not join the staff for a morning cup of tea.

Actually all these people are lonely souls and are to be pitied. *They are lonely not because they are not loved, but because they cannot love.* The happiness of love is our response to love. To know that we are loved without being able to respond to that love may flatter our vanity, but it cannot give happiness. Normal love is always a two-way traffic; and it not only enjoys the love given by the beloved, but finds its happiness in returning the love. Neurotic love is wholly egocentric, whereas true love is object-centred. Its joy lies in making the loved one happy, not in being made happy. Here, if I may digress for a moment, is where so many young people make their mistake in their approach to marriage. They look for someone who 'will make me happy', whereas the sign that one is in love is the tremendous desire to make that other person happy. The ideal marriage is that in which both partners are consciously and unconsciously motivated by the desire to make the other happy.

The neurotic need for affection, then, prevents the personal relationships, the intimate contacts in which happiness lives, moves and has its being, and in which the self realises itself as a harmonious whole. Happiness, remember, is a satisfied self, and not merely a gratified impulse, or desire. We may gratify an impulse or desire and regret it to the end of our days. We can never regret a moment's happiness; in that moment, however fleeting, the self as a whole has expressed and realised itself.

The Need for Social Status and Morbid Character-
   Structures

My own experience of neurotic troubles leads me to
believe that there are more morbid complexes and character-
structures connected with the need for social status than
any other of our needs. Let us remember that the indulgence of a perverted tendency will not of itself break anyone
down—nor for that matter will promiscuous sexual tendencies—nor will the expression of left-over infantile
behaviour-tendencies. Even the neurotic need for affection
will not necessarily break one down, although as long as it
is retained, there can be no happiness. Many perverts are
entirely free from neuroticism, and indeed are justified in
their own eyes that they are as entitled to their perverted
form of pleasure as normal people whose pursuit of pleasure
takes a normal form. It is not until our behaviour-tendencies
are in danger of thwarting our status that conflict begins
and the tendency to repression is set in motion; neuroticism
results. Unless the individual can rationalise his behaviour-
tendencies he is faced with the threat to his social status,
his self-respect, and the respect of others. Any threat to our
social status will be reacted to by a morbid defence reaction unless we have the necessary courage and faith to
face the situation and deal with it consciously. The well-
known inferiority complex, the lesser inferiority feelings,
and the self-consciousness experienced in company by
many people have their roots here. Any physical impair-
ment, lack of education or general culture in the individual
who has come into a class where education of a general
kind is expected to show in his manners and conversation,
marrying into a social class above one's upbringing, or
getting a position for which one is not really equipped—
all these can generate inferiority feelings and create morbid

character-structures of one kind or another. For instance, the lad with an undropped testicle becomes compelled to prove his masculine virility and may become a danger to society as well as to himself.

As an over-compensation for any of these 'inferiorities', the individual may generate a drive to be superior to others, and to get prestige or social recognition, and the character-structure created will depend on the manner in which he tries to get this superiority acknowledged. The dread of failure and humiliation is always an underlying emotional tone in the psychological make-up of these people. Very often there is the tendency to 'debunk' others, not uncommon in authors who have no creative power of their own. Historians of philosophy who could not construct a philosophy of their own will bring out the defects of all existing philosophies and fail to bring to their students' minds the value of any one philosophy. 'If you cannot emulate an author, then debunk him'—that seems to be their unconscious motive.

Dr. Horney[1] mentions three neurotic trends which I should say are the outcome of thwarted social status. These are all attempts to gain the desired prestige. *There is the definite craving for prestige, often, she says, accompanied by the craving for power. Friends are chosen for their prestige which can cover them with a sort of reflected glory.* One person I knew, who had married a step above her, made a great deal of the colonels, generals and other high ranking people her husband had to bring home in the course of his vocation. In her conversation with ordinary people she could not prevent herself monopolising the attention of her listeners to a catalogue of their honours, virtues, or whatever would impress them. These people must draw atten-

[1] 'Self-Analysis,' Chapter 2.

tion to themselves and excite envy or admiration; and, as there are many ways of doing that, the result may be a man who differs from everybody else, and gains a reputation for his independence of judgment and speech, when in reality he is compelled to differ and be different from anyone else. As in the case of the 'debunking' tendency, not a few writers have built up a good reputation by this compulsive tendency.

Two of the most interesting of these character-trends are those in which the individual has to live up to an inflated image of himself and whose 'happiness' depends on the admiration of himself by others. He must get others to think well of him. Alas, people do not admire us for imaged virtues or abilities, but for what we are.

On the other hand this drive for prestige and recognition may be the motive of ambition. Darwin tells us in his autobiography that he made up his mind to make a contribution to his subject—a laudable ambition which was more than fulfilled. The neurotic motive, however, is not to make a contribution to anything—although one may be made— but to surpass others, to be thought the best in the particular field. Such a motive will run through the whole of an individual's life, not merely his work. If he is married, he must get his wife and everyone else to believe that he is the best husband. If he is a preacher, then his people must not compare him with anyone else, except to his advantage. He gets what I have sometimes called a 'watch me' complex. He takes every opportunity to show people how much better he can do everything than everybody else. Naturally, in his subconscious mind he is never sure of himself. If a man is kind he has not to try to be kind, if he is a good husband he will not need to emphasise it. In such individuals who have managed to live without breaking under the strain of eternally trying to do something better than anyone else, there will be found an underlying anxiety and dread of failure—a dread which as often as not leads to failure as in the sportsman. Often these people have ability and achieve a good deal, but, as they cannot surpass everybody, they never get any happiness out of all their effort.

Need for Rational Unity and Morbid Character-Structures

The need for rational unity gives rise to some interesting character-trends. If an individual has started out in his life of thought with some intellectual pre-suppositions, or dogmas, first accepted in virtue of suggestibility and which at adolescence gave him a sense of intellectual security and unity, he may be compelled to develop logic-tight compartments through which these dogmas and pre-suppositions are kept proof against all rational argument. This is especially true of political and religious beliefs. This is the type of mind which accounts for men of great intellectual ability who never grow up either in their political or religious opinions and who, in particular, can hold on to articles of religion, the grounds for which are often very shaky. There are others whose beliefs really become undermined, but the unbelief is repressed and often then a breakdown results. For some reason or another such people cannot bear to lose the sense of rational unity. I had as a patient a clergyman who was held in very high regard in one branch of the Anglican Church. He became a chaplain in the first world war. Soon after demobilisation he developed a nervous symptom which expressed itself in the form that he felt sick at the altar especially if he were dispensing the sacrament of the Lord's Supper, or when he went into the pulpit to preach. He was never sure that he could carry out either of those duties without this horrible nausea. The root of the trouble was that while a chaplain he found that those who had 'partaken of the blood and body of our Lord' were neither braver, more courageous, nor were they better in conduct behind the lines than those who had not shared in the Eucharist. This created a doubt as to whether after all his high doctrines were really true and whether they really mattered for true religion. That doubt was repressed very largely because it would have meant a rethinking of his whole theological position, and he would certainly have lost the prestige he had in the branch of the Church whose doctrines he had been foremost in propagating and defending. There was an unconscious conflict between his wish to keep his status in the Church and the drive for rational unity.

Although the conflicts arising from the drive for rational unity do not as a rule lead to nervous breakdown, they can create a great deal of mental distress. Some people live very uncomfortably with a 'perhaps'. These painful religious doubts were more common in days when religious beliefs were more stable than they are now. Carlyle gives us the classic conflict in *Sartor Resartus* when the 'Everlasting no' was finally silenced. I am afraid, however, that if you listen you will hear it coming out in Carlyle's overstrong affirmations—to say nothing of his dyspepsia.

There we must leave the conflicts arising out of the thwarting of the fundamental needs. In our next lecture we shall see the conflicts which have their roots within conscience—the drive for moral unity. Just as the body strives for organic wholeness, so the soul of man cannot but strive for that wholeness in which a mature personality expresses itself and realises itself. Any threat to that wholeness at once sets up a conflict, and our reaction to that conflict determines our mental health and peace. We may face the conflict or unconsciously build a character-structure which defends us against the threat, but at the expense of personality and mental health. In virtue of what we shall see as the psycho-somatic unity of personality, our physical health can be affected and bodily functioning disturbed. In virtue of the need for others and for society, our personal and social relations may be disrupted. A man who cannot make friends or who is always choosing the wrong ones; the individual who is incapable of falling in love with the opposite sex, or, married, fears having children; an individual who cannot hold his job and yet is efficient, or who cannot make his home life happy is ill.[1] He is torn by unconscious conflicts of one kind or another; he has built up defences in the form of character-structures which are often contradictory and leave him with a sense of insecurity; he is conscious of unstable and conflicting emotions. In such the personality drive has failed. The will that cannot canalise the energy, emotions and ideas along self-chosen ends is weak, and its owner is left at the mercy of an infantile unconscious which drives him whither it will.

---

[1] Cf. 'Man, Morals and Society,' by Flügel, Chapter 7, for excellent illustrations.

THE ORIGIN AND DISSIPATION OF MORBID GUILT

I PROMISED in my last lecture that I would give special attention to the conflicts arising out of the need for moral unity. They are indeed the most severe as they involve, not merely fear of the loss of social, but of moral status. Any frustration of the drive for moral unity coming from within our personality sets up a threat both to our self-respect and to the respect of others for us.

Conflicts arising out of behaviour-tendencies, complexes or character-structures which the self has not been able to unify with conscience invariably produce guilt-feelings and also a strong tendency to self-punishment. Unfortunately, we cannot take the guilt-feelings as signs of repentance, for, as often as not, these guilt-feelings are a sign that the offending tendencies are very active, although repressed; there is no change of heart, and the guilt-feelings, by pre-occupying the individual's mind, act as a self-defence of a repetition of the prohibited behaviour. Guilt-feelings in my opinion are always morbid and a moment in the downward thrust of repression. They are generated by what I call 'the infantile conscience' and which the psycho-analysts term the 'super-ego'. Very often the guilt-feelings are displaced upon incidents or behaviour which could not possibly carry the amount of guilt from which these people suffer. Here is a good example of displacement and defence against the offending tendencies. A young woman came to see me who had very great difficulty in walking and who was almost consumed by a morbid sense of guilt. She was obsessed by an incident which happened in her school days. The teacher had been giving a lesson on chocolate-making. I imagine the chocolate makers gave the education authorities a supply of the materials for demonstration; among these materials were bars of chocolate. The various stages of manufacture were demonstrated right up to the shining bars of tempting chocolate. Two of the girls in the class, of whom my patient was one, became curious as to whether the bars of chocolate were real. At the interval they crept into the class-room and tasted the chocolate. The incident was really forgotten until confirmation. The vicar saw each candidate for confirmation, and asked them individually whether they would like to make their confession before the actual day of the ceremony and the taking of their first communion. My patient became full of guilt-feelings and they attached themselves to this old incident. She felt almost compelled to confess it, but resisted, and from that day the guilt-feelings increased. Finally, when she was about twenty, she fell ill. Analysis soon showed that the guilt belonged not to this incident, on which it had been displaced, but to other behaviour. Had this behaviour been confessed at first no doubt the good vicar would have helped the girl to dissipate the guilt and to bring the tendencies under self-control. Instead of that, the truly offending tendencies became repressed and anxiety and the peculiar form of walking were sufficient to protect her against behaviour which her conscience would have spontaneously condemned. Thus the guilt and the walking were defence reactions—plus self-punishment.

Sometimes the guilt becomes displaced on any trivial deviation from the path of perfection, while the behaviour-tendency which ought to be condemned, or controlled, is allowed full exercise without any sense of guilt at all.

Morbid guilt here is a screen diverting the patient's attention from what is really happening. Self-recriminations, the
finding of flaws within themselves, and strong self-punishment tendencies are always found in those with a capacity
for strong guilt feelings.

Guilt-feelings, we can take it, are always morbid, always
a moment in the downward thrust of repression, always a
sign that some conflict is not being faced. They always
prevent real moral insight into the true condition of the
individual. They are by no means confined to people who
break down. They are rife in all people in whom the infantile conscience still holds sway, or in whom it has not
been outgrown. Moral and spiritual scruples are bad companions, they give no peace, and they are always morbid.
Shame, regret, humility are the true signs of contrition;
they are genuine moral and spiritual emotions and they
are what we ought to experience on the realisation that we
have done, felt, or thought something morally reprehensible.
They are true moments of repentance, and the experience
of them tends to increase our moral insight about ourselves,
and naturally tends to modify the offending behaviour-
tendencies. Guilt feelings do not manifest sorrow for sin,
but only the fear of consequences. Shame, regret and
humility have no fear of consequences; they are the outcome of moral perception. Guilt-feelings are just a barrier
to the offending tendencies, a barrier behind which the
tendencies are active and thus keep the individual in a state
of moral and spiritual insecurity. True moral emotions
change our whole moral attitude to the offending tendencies. The old Church Fathers were right when they contended that a truly Christian repentance of a particular sin
meant that the temptation to that sin could not recur. The
strength of a temptation marks the degree to which the sin

has not been repented. The strength of our morbid guilt is the measure of the defences needed against the offending tendencies.

What, then, is the Origin of these guilt-feelings that can be such a disturbing factor in life, not only of the neurotic, but of those we should call normal? To answer we have to watch the development of conscience. Conscience, as we have seen, is the organ of the self's need for unity, the self's drive for moral wholeness. It is a function of the need for moral unity. *Its authority lies, not in the objective standard of the ideal, but in the fact that it co-ordinates and regulates our behaviour in the interest of the personality as a whole.* That authority is exerted within the field of the moral standards, consciously or unconsciously accepted. Conscience in itself is innate, the standards are derived from our parents, teachers and the community. It is for moral philosophy to examine the validity of the standards which prevail in a community and which the child internalises. Psychology is not altogether irrelevant here. If it cannot dictate to us what we ought to do, it can tell us whether our standards are trying to make us into something we can never become.

The Development of Conscience

Be that as it may, my task now is to show how the sense of guilt originates. We saw when dealing with the organising activity of the mind that from the beginning of the infant's life sense impressions become synthesised in perceptions; the emotions, impulses and ideas become organised within sentiments. In other words, the child's inner life is orientated in relation to external objects. Later, the child acquires abstract sentiments, such as the sentiment of beauty, or goodness or truth. How soon the child begins to have a moral sentiment it is difficult to say. Very quickly the child senses approval and disapproval, but this is not necessarily moral. The infant senses approval or disapproval from the attitude and behaviour of the mother; it learns to say 'sorry' or 'pardon' for some little breach of manners long before it has sensed moral approval or disapproval. Even when it senses the difference—that moral approval is qualitatively different from the approval given for some little trick it has learned, such as standing by itself, or walking, or on acquiring a new word—it still thinks of itself in terms of the third person. True moral feelings are certainly experienced in the child before self-consciousness and we know that sensual and hostility feelings can be repressed before self-consciousness, but that must be because they have been disapproved of severely and the child is afraid of some kind of punishment. With self-consciousness, however, the sense of moral approval and disapproval can be referred to the self, and the moral sentiments begin to organise the child's behaviour, and at this point it is possible for the child to begin to acquire a positive conscience. Before this the child is governed largely externally, and at first the child would be guided a great deal by prohibitions rather than positive directions. Like Socrates' 'daemon' conscience would appear as a check from within the child. Bergson begins his first chapter of his volume of *The Two Sources of Morality and Religion* by saying: 'The remembrance of forbidden fruit is the earliest thing in the memory of each one of us as it is in that of mankind. We should notice this, were not this recollection overlaid by others which we are most inclined to dwell upon. What a childhood we should have had if only we had been left to do as we pleased! We should have flitted from pleasure to pleasure. But all of a sudden an obstacle arose, neither visible nor tangible; a prohibition'.[1] Only by prohibitions is the mother able to teach the child at first, because the child cannot possibly form moral concepts. The child is thus guided wholly by approval and disapproval. However, he quickly senses the difference in the mother's disapproval of a breach of manners and of some misdemeanour in anything sexual or connected with the excretory functions. It is at this stage we see conscience, or what the psychoanalysts term the 'super ego', beginning to regulate the child's behaviour-tendencies and feelings. *The mother's prohibitions are internalised.* The mother cannot be with the child always; the now internalised prohibitions act in lieu of the mother's actual presence, and rise spontaneously to check the child when about to do something which, were the mother there, she would prohibit. Suppose a child is forbidden to take sugar or jam from the larder. Suppose further that the child finds itself in the larder and mother not there. It sees the desired sugar or jam and the natural impulse is to take some. The prohibitions regarding sugar and jam arise to check the child. If the prohibition is disobeyed, or the child has taken the sugar or jam before the prohibition had time to act, then the child is likely to experience uncomfortable feelings, in proportion as the prohibition was accompanied by an implicit threat of punishment or disapproval. Guilt-feelings will immediately arise, and the feelings may be so painful as to compel the child to confess; for confession invariably relieves guilt-feelings. Otherwise the child has to repress the painful feelings in order to appear innocent when the mother appears.

Now prohibitions extend to a great deal farther than taking sugar and jam, and indeed are far more severe in

[1] 'The Two Sources of Morality and Religion,' Chapter 1.

relation to other kinds of behaviour, e.g. hostility feelings, sensual acts, nakedness or curiosity. As I said before, the child senses a different attitude in the mother relating to these than to taking the sugar and jam or a breach of good manners. A great deal depends on the mother's attitude; if the mother herself has repressed feelings in regard to these things she is likely to be more severe on the child and transmit a greater sense of guilt than a mother who has an entirely rational attitude to the behaviour of children.

Thus guilt feelings have their origin in the activity of this prohibitive, infantile conscience or super ego. The danger of the prohibitive conscience is not so much its capacity to generate guilt-feelings, but its capacity to make the child repress its behaviour-tendencies, and also the guilt-feelings themselves. The result is that a barrier is erected in the child's mind against the offending tendencies and they are not allowed to rise into consciousness and then become controlled consciously. The prohibitions lie over against these tendencies daring them, as it were, to come into consciousness. *Hence the tendencies cannot become modified, but remain active in the unconscious mind in an infantile state of development.* If this prohibitive conscience is too strongly implanted there is a great danger that it will be carried over into adolescence and adulthood, and the boy and man will become more afraid of doing wrong than desirous of seeking the right and good. The conscience is unable to fulfil its function of co-ordinating and regulating the behaviour-tendencies according to some consciously chosen ideal. The conscience becomes an inner policeman, often a bully, keeping the personality in a state of moral division and moral immaturity. As long as the behaviour-tendencies are simply held by prohibitions, repressive forces are continuously active in the unconscious, and there will be a continuous sense of moral insecurity often shown in a fear of heights, or of falling, or, worst of all, in all kinds of moral scruples. Apprehensiveness, lack of concentration and guilt-feelings are likely never to be far away from the conscious field. There is unconscious preoccupation in defending the conscious mind against immature and rebellious impulses, and there is little chance of the individual acquiring true moral insight or positive moral sentiments which would spontaneously guide the behaviour-tendencies towards goals consistent with the mature mind. The fear of vice and wrong-doing becomes stronger than the love of virtue and right-doing.

We have said that every prohibition contains an implicit threat; the threat is, as a rule, vague and the child is left to imagine what would happen if the prohibition were disobeyed. The threat is embodied in the infantile conscience or super ego. The result is that the child is not only inwardly commanded not to disobey the prohibition, but experiences an impulse towards self-punishment.[1]

I saw one little child coming to get slapped; the same child used to bang its head against the wall when it did wrong. Sometimes children will threaten themselves with all sorts of punishment if they do the wrong thing again; 'paying forfeits' I sometimes call it. I had one patient in whom this tendency got so strong that she threatened herself with the thought that God would not forgive her, and thus got afraid of doing something that God could not overlook. I had another patient who had strong hostile feelings. These were met by an internalised prohibition which first came from a rather tyrannical father. The tension and guilt feelings generated by the prohibitive conscience could only get release by a threatening of herself with all sorts of self-

[1] Cf. 'Man, Morals and Society,' Flügel, Chapter 3 ff.

punishment, even to the extent of being denied any contact with God. It was more than once difficult to keep the patient from losing her job. She was more than sure she would be dismissed and unconsciously created situations in which the possibility was not imaginary. I had another who when she fell to her besetting sin used unconsciously to provoke a row with her mother on some very trivial matter. Apparently, once her mother was angry with her, the self-punishment tension was relieved and all was sunshine again until the next time. Fortunately, I was able to help her to get insight into the process and to take a more adult attitude to her besetting sin and her reaction to it when she did fall. The self-punishment can be inordinately harsh; for this reason psycho-analysts speak of the 'severity of the super ego'. That is also the reason why a great deal of the work of analysis has to be occupied in reducing the intolerance of the infantile conscience; for it is only when we have reduced this intolerance[1] that the work of re-education can begin. Both the demands and the threats of the prohibitive conscience are dynamic; if the demands are not met self-punishment becomes almost automatic.[2]

So far I have spoken as though the prohibitions of the infantile conscience were homogeneous. That is not the case. Contradictory demands or standards may be internalised. The prohibitions of the mother may be different from the prohibitions of the father; and those of teachers may be different from both. Then there are things which the child is not allowed to do which the parent actually does. For example a parent may be in the habit of swearing and the child be punished for any attempts to swear; many children cannot understand why they have to stay outside a public

[1] See 'Psycho-Analysis To-day', edited by Sandor Loraud, p. 57. (London: George Allen & Unwin Ltd.)
[2] Cf. 'Man, Morals and Society,' p. 52 f.

house while their parents go in to refresh themselves. They thus acquire the contradictory feeling about going into a public drinking place that it cannot be wrong and yet it is prohibited. We may get a patient who has been brought up in a rather strict home, but is sent to a school where the teachers have a much broader outlook on what is approved or disapproved. The child acquires a double standard which remains in a state of conflict. I had a patient, pagan in many ways so far as her unconscious is concerned, but puritanic in many other ways. The double standard never became reconciled, and even to the present day will manifest itself in her dreams. The contradictory nature of the prohibitions often leads to vacillation in moral affairs.

Now, while it is true that the moral education of children, and indeed (if Bergson is near the truth) moral consciousness, begins in a prohibition, from the very start parents and teachers, and especially religious teachers, should realise that their task is not to implant prohibitions against doing wrong, or of being 'naughty', but to develop a love for the good. *Goodness is not simply an absence of wrong-doing,* but a love of whatsoever things are good, honest, lovely and of good report. That love becomes a direction to the behaviour-tendencies, and that is what a positive conscience should be: a direction, a guide. It restrains us without repression, and compels us to think on what we are about to do. It makes possible deliberation. This is the adult positive conscience. It co-ordinates and regulates behaviour-tendencies towards the best; and it does this spontaneously. *Inclination and will become one; what we want to do and what we ought to do coincide. The Kantian antithesis between inclination and will is resolved in the new synthesis of inclination and will.*

The psycho-analysts have certainly helped us to understand the evil effects of the internalisation of the prohibitions of parents and teachers and how the ego-ideal imposed upon the child becomes embodied in the infantile conscience. But they have failed to show us how the prohibitive conscience must be converted into a positive conscience with its self-chosen ego-ideal, and self-chosen ends, and how that self-chosen ideal spontaneously controls and directs the behaviour-tendencies. They have shown, more than any other school, the evil effects in neurotic development of these internalised prohibitions which lie over against the growing personality. What we need to know now is how a child grows in moral stature without having to fight guilt-feelings and prohibitions at every turn. St. Paul's conversion was really a conversion from a prohibitive conscience, in which the prohibitions were re-enforced by the fear of the wrath of God, to a realisation that love is the fulfilling of the law. We have here again the problem of the 'once-born'; they seem to have grown up without the need for repression; and one can only say that, from a very early period of life, inclination and will have synthesised.

The positive conscience can be described in a sentence or two. It is like sign posts at the different cross-roads directing the driver towards his journey's end. A good driver simply keeps his eye on the number of the road into which he has to turn or to continue on. The prohibitive conscience instead of keeping the eye on the road on which the individual should go keeps watching the roads down which it must not go. Miss Petre, the Roman Catholic Modernist, tells how when she was learning to cycle she was inevitably drawn towards everything that would obstruct her path or throw her off her balance. Then an old Scotch gardener who was teaching her said: 'Don't look where you don't want to go; keep your eye on where you want to go'.[1] There could be no sounder advice to a parent or teacher who has the moral care of children. Teach them to stop looking where you don't want them to go and direct their attention to where you want them to go. 'Walk in the Spirit', says St. Paul and 'you will not fulfil the lusts of the flesh'; 'Love me and you will keep my commandments', says our Lord. The moral sign of a mature Christian is the positive conscience, organising behaviour-tendencies, impulse, emotions spontaneously towards the moral goals in which the personality grows into a harmonious, moral whole.

Conscience should be the ally of the moral life, not its policeman. Its function is to co-ordinate and regulate behaviour-tendencies by the idea of the best, not to bully us into a fear of doing wrong and through that fear repress the offending tendencies. The true educator will see to it that duty is not a burden to be carried, but a guide-post to conscience. Self-control may be a necessity, and is often a virtue; but it implies that we have behaviour-tendencies that need watching. Self-possession is what we should help our children to acquire. In self-possession our impulses, emotions and ideas are ours to send them where we will. It is the mark of a personality whose behaviour-tendencies are organised within sentiments in harmony with conscience— the sex-impulses organised within our moral sentiments or within a love sentiment for a member of the other sex; hostility impulses at the direction of a positive conscience.

We have seen that many character structures of a morbid kind are acquired if the need for love is thwarted in any way; e.g. the neurotic need for affection, the neurotic need for approval and the fear of disapproval. Dr. Karen Horney lays stress on two neurotic trends which I believe

[1] 'My Way of Faith.'

to be acquired in defence against these guilt-feelings. They are always the sign that the conscience is infantile and prohibitive and that the individual is ruled by moral imperatives, which lie over against his behaviour-tendencies keeping them in check, but never modifying them. The more important of the two which she mentions is, 'The Neurotic Need for Perfection and Unassailability'.[1] This is really a defence against tendencies which threaten the moral integrity of the individual. It is not confined to people who have broken down; often it is mistaken for a sign of high character. Always I have found this character-trend to be accompanied by a strong tendency to morbid moral scruples. It is a rigid structure and has invariably a religious sanction behind its demands. It drives the individual relentlessly towards an ego-ideal that has never been integrated with the personality. The ideal itself is more negative than it is positive. In other words, *it is a case of the individual ceaselessly trying not to be bad rather than of any drive towards a virtuous character.* Any deviation from this negative ideal brings self-recriminations, and these are accompanied by painful guilt-feelings. This drive is invariably a defence reaction against strong sensual and hostile tendencies. It is analogous to the tendency towards a strict religious orthodoxy which we find in some people who dare not allow a doubt to enter their conscious mind, lest their whole religious creed crumble. Their religious faith is really a defence reaction against scepticism. When one digs a little below the surface one finds in the perfectionist a very great envy (naturally disguised) of those who can sit loose to their conscience. Their envy is almost indistinguishable from jealousy, and this comes out in their readiness to criticise others who are less strict in their lives. *They envy the moral*

(1) 'Self-Analysis,' Chapter 2.

freedom which they fear. Their criticism is really a very subtle way of abusing their own reprehensible, repressed tendencies without having to reproach themselves. They cannot always escape their own repressed self-criticism, and this comes out in a compulsive tendency to find flaws in themselves; and, what is probably worse still, the tendency to moral scruples, which pester them at all times. Miss Petre has well called these scruples 'spiritual vermin.' She herself suffered from this perfectionist trend between the years of ten and thirteen. I can confirm from clinical experience that it is just at this age, early puberty, when this perfectionist trend tends to get rooted.

I cannot define the term 'scruple' better than Miss Petre does: 'A "scruple" means strictly any form of anxiety, sensitiveness and niceness in action. In religion it has come to mean such an obsessive dread of sin as leads the mind to fear its very shadow, to distrust one's power of avoiding it; and to feel guilty where no guilt is.' She adds truly: 'But this unreasoning dread of sin is not—certainly in my experience—inspired by an excessive wish to do right, but by a terror of doing wrong because of the awful consequences thereof'.[1]

Miss Petre thinks that the morbid tendency is never found apart from belief in mortal sin and eternal damnation. My experience with patients who have really broken down under the impossible perfectionist strain is that the majority of them do hold these beliefs; but there are others with strongly repressed hostile tendencies to whom this would not apply. Where the perfectionist trend is a defence reaction against sensual feelings and tendencies, it is invariably tinged with religious fear, and that certainly adds to the misery of the patient.

---

[1] 'My Way of Faith,' Chapter 3.

The hostile feelings of the perfectionist are as much feared as sensual sin and its shadow. They are accentuated by the continuous fight with the 'spiritual vermin' or scruples. The repressed hostile feelings are over-compensated by an excessive fear of having hurt someone; or the patient dreads that he, or she, might do so. I had one patient who, if she gave her charwoman a tin of fruit or meat, would be in misery for days lest it might cause food-poisoning; another who could not dress a wound without the fear that she had not been careful enough and that septic poisoning might set in; another who happened to leave her direction signal on her car up and twice had to go to the chief-constable's department to be reassured that no accident had occurred—in fact, she would not leave the office until she had seen the chief superintendent. Miss Petre herself tells us that she wrote in agony to a shopkeeper to tell her that she had drunk out of a ginger-beer bottle while she had a sore throat, and pleaded with her to have the bottle disinfected lest it cause the death of someone.

Many of these people need continually to be reassured that God would forgive them even if they did commit the most horrible of sins—which indeed they are incapable of committing. Often they have to propitiate their infantile prohibitive conscience by paying all sorts of 'forfeits,' sometimes at great inconvenience—the denial of simple pleasures, the forgoing of a holiday, the refusal to buy themselves some needed garment.

It is interesting to note how Miss Petre was cured of her 'spiritual vermin'. Her confessor 'forbade her all examination of her conscience, and the least mental reference to sin in any form for a whole year.' She had sufficient strength of purpose to obey and was cured. Only occasionally did she suffer afterwards. One had to remember in regard to

Miss Petre that doubt of the dogmas of her church would be treated as mortal sin; and I infer that even at the early age in which she was subject to these moral scruples already religious doubts were active in her subconscious mind.

The one real cure for this horrible character-trend is to help the individual to realise the nature of their ego-ideal; that their over-righteousness is a compensation and a defence against tendencies which have never been faced; then the infantile conscience must be transformed into an adult positive conscience.

The second character-trend which afflicts those with a prohibitive conscience unduly active is, as Dr. Horney puts it, 'The need to restrict life within too narrow limits.' Here again moral scruples are apt to complicate matters. The fear, however, is not in this case fear of hurting people, nor even a fear of sin in the perfectionist manner, but scruples as to what should be permitted in regard to personal pleasures. An illustration will help us here. A friend of mine had to travel a good distance by car to see a brother. He stopped by the way to have lunch. He had a good lunch and tipped the waiter. Then for the rest of the afternoon made himself miserable because he had spent what could have been given to the missionary society.

The restrictions, however, do not limit themselves to a supposed extravagance; they extend to the whole field of life. Ambitions and desire must be kept within strict limits and no advancement of any kind must be sought—indeed must be avoided. I have a patient who has the greatest difficulty in powdering her nose; and she would not dream of putting herself forward in any social contacts such as a Church committee. She must always take a back seat. It is not humility. She is envious of those who can do these things; she dare not, because her conscience would come down on her at once. She is conscious, ever since she was confirmed, of trying to be 'goody-goody'; and yet is conscious all through that she gets the most horrible hostile thoughts regarding people; and for this she punishes herself by more restrictions. Pleasure for pleasure's sake would to her be a sin. She is in love with a boy friend, but she dare not enjoy her love for him or his love for her. You can see at once that such a person can never get that real piety which is the true basis of personal religion. Miss Petre defines true piety as 'that joy and delight in fulfilling religious duties above the sense of obligation.' She contends that this piety is what has kept her still attached to her Church in spite of all her religious doubts. From a sense of obligation she would have gone to Mass, catechism, confession and communion; but ever since childhood she had this over-plus of real delight in all her religious duties, the duties she would have fulfilled as being expected of a child of the Church. Her duties were thus joys, and never a compulsion. They were directions spontaneously obeyed.

Here is the essential difference between one who has a compulsive tendency to restrict life within narrow limits and the normal person. The one is driven from behind, the other is pulled by an ideal freely and spontaneously accepted. Normal virtue will see self-sacrifice, not as a virtue, but sometimes as a necessity; a humble man will never refuse to be conspicuous in a good cause; and a sensible woman will make her personal appearance flow from her self-respect. Self-criticism will be constructive, correcting faults and giving confidence; whereas self-recrimination is destructive both of moral insight and moral confidence. In other words, self-criticism will be the outcome of the need for moral unity and moral insight and not a defence reaction to guilt-feelings generated by a prohibitive conscience.

People with either, or both, of these character-structures need to be reminded of the Scriptural injunction: 'Be not righteous overmuch.' They must acquire what one writer has called 'a resting point of satisfaction'.[1] None of us is satisfied with our achievements. We are all conscious of having had opportunities of which we have made too little; or seen them too late to take advantage of them. The perfectionists and the restrictionists are not satisfied with that; they must needs mourn the failure to achieve the impossible; they attempt to make of themselves what nature never meant them to become; and to achieve results for which they have neither the knowledge nor the talents.

These are the types that tend to develop physical symptoms of one kind or another which serve to screen the fact that they have escaped from the impossible demands upon themselves. They are like a golfer who secretly believes that he can really play to half his handicap; and will occasionally challenge a much better player, even a scratch man, only to find that on the day he has to play he has wakened up with an attack of lumbago! That allows him to keep his phantasy and at the same time provides him with a nice escape from humiliation!

Fortunately such patients are not too difficult to treat. Their tendencies are not too deeply repressed, and if they are willing to accept their limitations and live within them they can live a happy, contented and useful life.

Unfortunately, I have no time to deal with the complications which arise when individuals have contradictory character-structures. One may get a business man with a very strong exploiting tendency. Such a structure determines

---

[1] 'Psychology in General Practice,' edited by Alan Moncrieff, p. 86.

that he will see every situation where he may exploit for gain. At the same time he may have a strong prohibitive conscience which is ready to generate guilt immediately he attempts to exploit the situation. He wonders how other business men can do this or that and 'never turn a hair,' whereas he, poor fellow, just simply dare not.

Again, we may get a person with a strong tendency to remain inconspicuous; and yet with fierce ambitions to be somebody. Under the perfectionist screen you will almost invariably find strongly repressed hostile and sensual tendencies. The individual with a neurotic need to be loved has a morbid tendency to feel hostile to the very person he wants to love him.

No matter what the source of the conflict or the nature of it, the ultimate root of the trouble lies in the inability of the self to order its own life. The self is unable to canalise its energy, its emotions, and its ideas along the line of its own self-chosen channels. We may say, for the sake of simplification, that the Id is too strong for the Ego, or that the inclinations of the Ego are too strong for the rational control of the self; but it all comes back to the self. *After all, the tensions of the unconscious and the inclinations of complexes or character-structures can only solicit us, they need not coerce us. The final factor in any failure to achieve personality is the weakness of the self.* The controlling factors in our lives must be conscious, positive and free from fear. The self has to be liberated both from the threatenings of an infantile, prohibitive conscience, and ego-centred impulses and character-structures, which would either lead to uncontrolled pleasures, or to defence-formations against the unorganised tendencies. Character-structures should be the outcome of a love of virtue, and not acquired through a fear of vice. A man's conscience should express his freedom, not his slavery. Otherwise, at the least he will suffer from a continuous pervasive anxiety; at the worst he will never be free from fear and guilt-feelings. Only as we develop a positive conscience that becomes our guide, our friend, a bulwark against offending behaviour-tendencies within us can we get free from morbid guilt and live at peace with man, with God, and, above all, with ourselves.

LECTURE 5

SPIRITUAL HEALING

WE have now seen that in dealing with the individual we
are dealing with a whole—a self, a subject, a soul. It is a
something that you cannot explain in biological terms; it
can only be expressed in spiritual or moral terms. Every
need, biological or personal, may become a personal end
and, in so far as the personality-needs become personal
ends, we are on the way to realising our personality as a
whole.

I have shown that the springs of behaviour lie in the
fundamental needs of the organism and the personality; we
have seen something of the processes by which our inner
life is organised or disorganised. It would be a mistake,
however, to suppose that we could explain personality in
terms of its parts. The self is not a mere integration of parts
or processes. Indeed, the self *is* the integrating principle of
the parts. In other words, the self is not a mathematical
unity, but a dynamic unity; that is why it is subject to conflict, even to division. To the degree that dynamic unity is
not attained there is conflict; the self is pulled in opposite
directions by its own inclinations. When we talk of conflict,
we must not think of the self as a spectator watching something outside itself. In so far as it cannot integrate its desires,
its wishes, its emotions, its thoughts and behaviour-tendencies with the conscious or unconsciously accepted standards
of conscience it becomes ill, in exactly the same way as it is
the life that is in danger when the lungs or heart cannot
function properly. And just as medicine attempts to remove

hindrances to the balanced working of the organism so as to allow the life-processes to animate the organs freely and healthfully, so the healer of the soul tries to help the self to resolve its conflicts, integrate its experiences and freely move towards its prospective aim.

Our problem, in this lecture, is to answer the question of methods of helping the self to regain its dynamic unity when it has become divided by conflicts. If, as we saw in the last lecture, we can get the child's wants to coincide with what is really satisfying to his needs, there should be no conflict. Were that happy stage reached in education then our whole problem would be that of directing the child to the best means of attaining his ends or of helping him to overcome the external difficulties to attaining his ends. Alas! The difficulties are within the child. Incompatible ends are soliciting him from within. Somehow, the child has to get rid of the tensions within himself. Here is father demanding that the child do one thing and the inclinations of the child solicit his attention for a quite opposite thing. Something in him wants to obey father, or fears the punishments of the father or even his disapproval. Tension is set up, the tension may become unbearable. He may then obey with a grudge; the grudge gets repressed; he does what his father wants him to do; but the repressed grudge sets up a new tension. He may then become irritable; the father frowns on that. The grudge may become more deeply repressed. There you have the beginnings of a rebel character-structure. He then begins to hide wishes or acts which he knows the father would disapprove; he appears one thing to his father and another to himself. He may manage to hide his hostile feelings entirely from himself and seemingly become the most compliant of sons.

You may rightly ask me how it is possible for a self-conscious individual to hide from himself what his real feelings are.   Here in the ordinary course of things I should have had to go into all the defence-mechanisms by which we rationalise our actions, displace our emotions or over-compensate for hidden tendencies. That I did in my last 'Tate Lectures,' and you will find them in the little volume 'Nervous Disorders and Character'; and there I must leave it.   At the moment we are only concerned as to methods by which we attempt to cure the symptoms and heal the whole man of his psychological disease.

There are patients with whom we can do nothing at all. Freud said they suffered from Narcissistic Neuroses. We can look over the wall; we can see what is going on, but nothing we can do at the present in the way of analysis seems to be able to reach the self to whom is given the power of insight. Their capacity for inner perception seems to be utterly impaired.

Here is one case: the patient was a man in his forties. He complained bitterly that he was growing shorter every day.   Analysis quickly showed that he had been morally shrinking for a long time.   His religious and moral ideals were kept in a logic tight compartment and exercised little or no criticism of his phantasies, which were of a highly immoral nature.   True moral criticism of himself had been entirely repressed.   Then something was casually said by a traveller in his business which apparently struck home to his infantile conscience and tended to reveal himself to himself.   In other words, some sort of self-criticism attempted to function, but instead of accepting the self-criticism and correcting or modifying the phantasy tendency, it was repressed.   The self-criticism which he refused to accept by his conscious mind came back to him through his delusion that he was growing shorter every day. His delusion was the displacement upon his body of the repressed feeling of a shrinking soul. Unfortunately, the delusion had become so deeply rationalised that there was no hope of a cure. When I attempted to get him to face the real thing which was shrinking, extreme hostile feelings arose in his mind. There was no cure; his condition was now psychotic and not psycho-neurotic; in other words, insight had become impaired beyond recovery.

Even when we can reach the self with its insight and can bring the whole trouble into consciousness, the individual is not necessarily cured. Character-structures have to be changed; a new habitual centre from which action proceeds has to be formed; round that centre sentiments have to be organised; perhaps new sentiments have to be created.

A normal individual has besetting sins which he knows as such. He knows they can disturb his personal relationships and he knows the dangers involved. But that, alas! does not of itself create the repentance which changes a man's self or soul. What astonishes us is the number of business men, professional men and adolescents of both sexes who can risk their whole reputation and their career —to say nothing of their character—for the twinge of a nerve, a sensual thrill, or a bit of money. There is no class immune. In these the conscience becomes repressed. Then at the slightest hint of being found out, they crack. The tendencies become repressed, the conscience comes to the surface and symptoms develop. Instead of being distressed about the tendencies, they become afraid of the asylum. The fear of insanity is simply the fear of their divided soul, whose tendencies and passions the self is afraid it cannot control.

Our problem now is: how do we get at the unconscious tendencies so as to bring them into consciousness? And how do we dissipate the anxiety and guilt or get rid of the symptoms?

In the first place we may attack the symptoms, paying little attention to the causative factors. This was the method of Coué: suggestion. That it is often successful I know from experience. Indeed, with very young people it is the method I use. They are too young for analysis. To give one illustration: she was a young girl of fourteen who was referred to me by her doctor, after he had tried everything he knew to cure her. She had half a dozen very painful sores in different parts of her body, one unsightly hole in the centre of her forehead. All of these sores had been created by scratching and picking. When the doctor managed to heal one sore she quickly found another spot to scratch; the forehead had been in this condition for a long time. I did not attempt to give much enlightenment on psycho-analytic lines, although it was obvious that the compulsive tendency was rooted in an infantile sexual tendency and involved self-punishment for repressed exhibitionism. I did try to make her realise that it was an infantile left-over, like a child retaining its fondness for the comforter long after it was necessary. All I did over a fairly long period was to suggest while she was in a hypnogogic state that she was becoming deeply interested in having a nice clean skin. Within a reasonable time the scratching stopped and rubbing was substituted; then finally that disappeared and the sores healed completely.

How dangerous blind suggestion can be I can attest from my own personal experience. My own boy when about seven or eight years of age was subject to attacks of earache which I easily removed by suggestion. Then I came home one week-end after being away lecturing to find that he had had a very severe attack and the ear was discharging. I told him I should have to take him to the specialist and he pleaded that I should give him some suggestion so that the doctor would not hurt him. When the specialist was examining him for mastoid he found that, no matter what he did to see whether there was any pain, nothing happened. Finally the doctor suspected I had given the child suggestion and asked me to remove its effects. In less than a minute the slightest pressure of the doctor's finger drew cries of pain. Actually there was a severe mastoid pain inhibited through suggestion and an immediate operation had to be performed.

Suggestion is only safe when it is applied with knowledge of what lies behind the symptoms. It should not be substituted for medical treatment of an organic disease, nor should it be applied in anxiety unless the causes of the anxiety are known. As Dr. William Brown has contended, suggestion should always be accompanied by analysis.

So far for the first method. The second method is the appeal to reason and the attempt to reassure the patient. It is the method we all use with our children's fears and even our friends'. It has, however, been reduced to a scientific system by Dubois. Persuasion plays a great part in all methods, and to some extent we all use it. Like the other systems, it can claim cures. Probably the system uses more analysis than it knows. After all, we have to give reasons and you cannot give them without knowing something of the underlying causes of the trouble.

The third method we must consider is that of Psychoanalysis. Freud was nothing if not a scientist. He believed that the causes of all neurosis must be looked for in childhood's experiences, and he was convinced that the trouble had its roots in some aberration of the sex impulses or in repressed hostility.

Beginning with the attempt to understand the systems of the psychotic, the obsessive fears and compulsive acts of the psycho-neurotic, Freud found the explanation in the unconscious and irrational elements in the make-up of personality. Along with Breuer, he was convinced that if he could make his patients recall the childish experiences which had been repressed and abreact the emotions these experiences had generated the patient would lose his symptoms. Hypnotism was the first method he employed to make the unconscious conscious. He soon found that not every patient could be hypnotised, and he devised his psycho-analytical technique of free association, in the belief that these associations would lead to the causes of the neuroticism. Free association is possible only on the condition that the patient will overcome the resistances of the moral inhibitions to the associations, and will pass no moral judgments on the 'wishes' or ideas he finds coming into consciousness. To the degree that these moral judgments and inhibitions are resisted, the sooner will the free associations bring up the disturbing factors and the sooner will the symptoms disappear.

Freud's interest was in psychiatry rather than in general psychology. His interest lay in psycho-pathology, in finding the mental causes for mental disturbances, and, apart from the great contribution of his technique, he opened up a wide field of investigation into mental processes. There can be no question to those familiar with pre-Freudian pyscho-pathology about the revolution in psychiatry which the new methods and new concepts created. Practically all schools of psychiatry and psychotherapy follow some form of psycho-analysis, even when they differ strongly about the fundamental concepts of Freud.

Freud's interest in dreams arose because his patients

complained of the terrifying nature of their dreams, and the anxiety and sweats with which these were accompanied. He came to the conclusion both by a study of his patients' dreams, and his own, that the dream was a 'wish fulfilment', and in neurotics this wish fulfilment was generally of a sexual nature. He believed that in sleep the repressing forces are somewhat in abeyance and the repressed wishes took their chance to reach consciousness. The distorted nature of dreams he accounted for on the hypothesis that the repressing forces were not altogether relaxed and, to evade the 'censor', the latent motives of the dream were disguised by various dream mechanisms, such as symbols, condensation, displacement and secondary elaboration. Thus the manifest content of the dream, i.e. the dream as remembered, had to be interpreted in order that the latent dream thoughts or wishes could be understood. To dreams he applied with great success his method of free association. The patient was asked to give the associations that came into his mind relative to the various parts of the dream, and it was these associations which gave the meaning to the dream. Many of the symbols in dreams he found were common to all dreamers, expecially those connected with sexual activity and the genitalia. His volume on dreams brought him to the forefront of investigators. To the end he believed that the dream, interpreted by free association, was 'the royal road to the unconscious'.

There were many, such as Jung and Rivers, who did not accept his idea that every dream could be interpreted as a wish-fulfilment of a childish nature. Rivers in his *Conflict and Dream* showed that many dreams were really an attempt to find a solution of a present problem and had no elements leading to repressed experiences of childhood. Jung found that many dreams showed not only the present conflict in the dreamer's mind but also tended to reveal a way by which self-development of the individual could take place. Nevertheless, none questioned the significance of the dream as a method of getting to know the hidden and unconscious factors in the patient's illness.

As I have said, Freud made a purely scientific approach to the problems of emotion and behaviour. Behaviour was essentially something to be understood and not something to be morally appraised or blamed. Naturally this led him to formulate psychological concepts to explain the dynamics of behaviour. His psychology is essentially a psychology of motivation. It is his concepts and not his analytical technique which form the bone of contention between the psycho-analytical school and all other schools of dynamic psychology.

The first of his concepts as we have already hinted, was that of the 'unconscious'. His patients, he could see, were perfectly unaware of the motivations of their behaviour or feelings. Neither philosophers nor psychologists[1] took kindly to the concept of unconscious ideas and wishes. They were already familiar with the idea of the unconscious in philosophy, and James had familiarised them with the subconscious and co-conscious of Morton Prince. Freud's conception was entirely different. Ideas and wishes of which the individual was entirely unaware were determining his behaviour and feelings. The fruitfulness of the concept is witnessed to by the help it has given in the understanding of both normal and morbid processes. Freud showed in his *Psycho-pathology of Every-day Life* that slips of the tongue, forgetfulness (which is very different from normal forgetting), errors in thought, speech and action, are not chance occurrences, but motivated from the unconscious.

[1] Cf. 'Nervous Disorders and Character,' McKenzie, p. 45 ff.

From all this Freud inferred that psychic processes are determined and that these determine behaviour. His logic here is doubtful. It is true that our psychic processes are determined, and that the behaviour of the neurotic and psychotic is determined is probably true. But we cannot deduce from that, as Freud does, that conscious process cannot influence psychic process or behaviour. When Freud speaks of psychic processes as being determined he means that they are determined by the past from the unconscious. The Gestalt school is nearer the truth in its assertion that at any given moment the past or early habits are just one factor in a, large system of forces, and that individual behaviour may be determined by goals whose realisation lies in the future. Freud's psychological determinism goes on the assumption that consciousness is always under the control of the unconscious. But, as John MacMurray[1] has pointed out, this places the analyst in the dilemma that if his theory is true his practice must be impossible, for the whole purpose of the practice is to bring the unconscious under the control of the conscious. Unless that is the aim of the practice there would be no sense in undertaking an analysis.

Nevertheless, the criticisms that may be brought against Freud's doctrine of psychological determinism do not logically detract from his findings that unconscious factors are at work as forces in our conscious behaviour. That they determine neurotic symptoms, such as irrational phobias, compulsive acts, like the washing of hands to get rid of a sense of guilt, or obsessive thoughts, no psychologist who has experience of clinical work could possibly deny. Freud was right in claiming that we cannot determine what will come into our conscious mind; but he failed to realise

---

[1] 'Boundaries of Science,' p. 176 f.

that what we shall do with it once it is there is determined by other processes than unconscious ones. I may, for example, experience an irrational irritability with my students in the class-room, but whether I shall express that irritability in words or actions should be perfectly under my control. I may be conscious of a perfectly irrational tendency to go to the devil, but I needn't and indeed wouldn't. In other words, determinism does not extend to the conscious. Choice is a conscious act, and our reasons for our choice need not be 'rationalisations'. Certainly there is a cause for my choice of one alternative rather than the other, but I am aware of why I prefer the alternative I have chosen. There is no such thing as a causeless act. Freedom, from the psychological point of view, is just our capacity to determine our reactions to what comes into our mind; or, to put it another way, our capacity to choose among alternatives from conscious reasons and on rational grounds.

If Freud's concept of the *unconscious* was at first unacceptable to many, that of 'repression' has created a good deal of confusion. Even today there are many writers who seem unable to differentiate repression from 'suppression' and 'self-control'. Freud's own definition is perfectly clear: 'The essence of repression lies simply in the function of rejecting and keeping something out of consciousness'. Doctor David Yellowlees gives the simplified definition that repression is a refusal to see something and not a refusal to do something. Dr. Rivers spoke of 'witting repression' and 'unwitting repression'. We are all familiar with the process of trying to keep something unpleasant from our conscious mind, e.g. some conscious worry or anxiety, because it is distracting our attention from our work; this is 'witting repression' according to Rivers. In

time the witting repression becomes automatic and unconscious and thus 'unwitting'. To Freud all repression was
unconscious.

Two questions arose for Freud from the facts of the unconscious wish, idea or emotion, and the process of repression by which they were made unconscious. 1, What is
it that we repress? 2, Why do we repress? The answer to
the first question which Freud gave was: 'some form of
infantile sexuality', or incipient incestuous wish formed
during the Oedipus period of childhood, i.e. during the
period when the attachment of the boy to the mother and
the girl to the father is very close. In his later thought Freud
recognised the presence of hostile wishes aroused and repressed during the oral stage, if for any reason the child
found difficulty in taking its feed; or at the anal stage, when
the child is being taught habits of cleanliness; or at the
genital stage, when the child becomes interested in its own
body and bodily sensations. Any frustration of sexual
interest or of the hunger appetite could arouse intense
hostility.

The answer he gave to the second question was that repressed wishes or emotions are contrary to the prohibitions
of the 'super-ego' or the childish conscience and unacceptable to the conscious image or 'ego-ideal' which the individual must live up to, and which he is expected to live up
to by parents, teachers and society.

None of the psycho-analytical doctrines aroused more
opposition than that of 'infantile sexuality'. What is called
the 'Personal Unconscious', i.e. the strivings, ideas, impulses and emotions repressed in experience, was for Freud
nothing but the product of the tensions created by infantile sexuality and aggression. All failure to adjust to reality
on the part of the self, all abnormality in behaviour or

H

emotion had their roots here. Hence the necessity for 'deep analysis', or 'depth psychology' if a cure was to be effected.

It was on this doctrine that Jung and Adler broke away from Freud. Jung believed that every breakdown was due to failure to meet present problems; it was a present situation that had to be analysed and faced, and not simply a sexual problem which had its roots in infantile sexuality or childish experiences. He refused to accept the Freudian concept of sexual libido as the dominating urge of life, as being too narrow. Libido to Jung is the general conational endeavour of the personality as a whole, and energises all our interests, not merely the sexual. Adler, on the other hand, paid little attention to the unconscious and, for him, sexual difficulties were secondary. He emphasised the aggressive impulses and thought that we are all dominated by the 'will to power', so that any frustration of that (such as some inferiority) could give rise to the failure to adjust one's self to life. Jung believed that the differences between himself and Freud go back to basic assumptions and, unlike both Adler and Freud, he refused to be convinced that man can be explained in terms of one fundamental urge. He did not doubt that there are individuals who can be explained in terms of Freudian or Adlerian psychology; there are people with infantile left-overs and those who can only be explained in terms of the struggle for superiority, but he declined to see normal man as necessarily dominated by either. To Jung the conflict is between biological needs and the drive for the realisation of the spirit;[1] and instead of seeing religion as an illusion, as Freud does, he saw it as the way man has always used to lessen as well as to resolve the conflicts which disturb his soul.

We are not specially concerned with these differences

[1] Cf. 'The Psychology of C. G. Jung,' by Dr. Jolen Jacobi, p. 61.

between the various schools of psychotherapy except in so far as they lead to differences of method of treatment. Actually there is not a great deal of difference in the methods of any of the great schools which owe their existence to Freud. Jung and Adler employed the method of free association, they both attached significance to dreams; but they both made the analysis a much more co-operative affair than did the orthodox psycho-analyst, whose method is simply to allow the patient to talk interminably with little explanation. All the schools, however, attempt to interpret the symbolisation of inner difficulties, and to explain the mechanisms by which the patient defends himself against undesirable tendencies.

It would take us too far afield to enter into the fundamental differences between those three great psychologists. Jung especially differs from Freud in his conception of the self or spirit. It is the 'indispensable formative power in the world of drives'. It is *sui generis* and is not to be explained in terms of sublimation. It is when this formative principle is thwarted that trouble begins.

The English school of psychiatrists approach the problems of neurosis along the middle of the road. They take everything that will help them to understand their patients and relieve the symptoms. Apart from Ian Suttie and Dr. Rivers there has been little or no attempt to work out theories of their own. Dr. MacCurdy's *Psychology of Emotion* criticises Freud, but could hardly be said to be anything more than an attempt to throw light on the origin and nature of emotion from a study of the Manic-Depressive varieties of neurosis and psychosis.

On the other hand, Dr. Karen Horney[1] of America has

---

[1] 'New Ways in Psycho-Analysis'; 'The Neurotic Personality of Our Time'; 'Self-Analysis,' and 'Inner Conflict'—all published by Kegan Paul.

worked out a theory in her four volumes which demanded new concepts. She was a strict Freudian psycho-analyst for fifteen years, but had increasingly found that Freud's concepts just would not fit her patients. In contrast to Freud's *complexes* she lays stress on *Neurotic Character-trends*. These, she believes, are acquired to ward off basic anxiety which arises from the feeling of insecurity created by the child's situation as a whole. She lays great emphasis on *The Need for Affection*, and in this aspect of her teaching comes near to the position of Dr. Suttie. Dr. Horney does not deny that there are patients who have traumatic experiences such as Freud enumerated, but it is the life situation and our reactions to that which are the important factors for our understanding of neurotic conflict. In my own experience I have found her findings very fruitful in the understanding of certain types of patients.

Allied to Dr. Horney's position is that of Erich Fromm of America. In his *Fear of Freedom* and *Man for Himself* he attempts to show that 'the key problem of psychology is that of the special relatedness of the individual toward the world and not that of satisfaction or frustration of this or that instinctual need *per se*'. He believes that man has less structural adjustment at birth than any other animal; consequently there is more flexibility in his behaviour-tendencies. To him the concept of instinct provides very little explanation of man's behaviour patterns. Man's problem is one of adaptation to cultural standards instilled first in the home, then school, and finally, in the larger social environment. This adaptation may be either of two kinds. There is 'static' adaptation which makes no demand for a change of character. He instances the Chinaman coming to America, who has to become adapted to American habits of eating with knives and forks and to new foods.

In adapting himself to these new ways and habits he does not need to acquire new drives. A 'dynamic' adaptation, on the other hand, means that something happens within the individual; it is more than the acquring of a new habit. Here he instances the boy who adapts himself to a strict or threatening father. He adapts himself by *submitting* to his father because of fear, but while adapting himself by submission he may acquire hostility which he dare not express; it becomes repressed but remains dynamic in the unconscious, and can set up new anxieties and certainly new character-structures, such as those outlined by Dr. Horney. Like Karan Horney, he believes that we seek consciously or unconsciously a sense of security; and if we cannot adapt ourselves to the home standards of the cultural standards we tend to seek roundabout ways of warding off the sense of insecurity or the sense of sin. The conflict, as was implied in the quotation from him, is that between the nature of man and the cultural standards; in other words, our cultural standards attempt to make man what he was never intended to become.

Submission, according to Fromm, is not the only way of dynamically adapting ourselves to our social environment. There may be a 'spontaneous relationship to man and nature, a relationship that connects the individual with the world without eliminating his individuality'. This kind of adaptation involves the integrated and total personality. Man's problem seems to be: What shall I do with my freedom? He may fear it and submit, or he may use it to make this spontaneous relationship with man and nature and lose his sense of insecurity and aloneness and consequently his anxiety, and then find his life expressing itself in love and productive work. He will love himself as well as others, for these are not alternatives.

In both Karen Horney and Fromm there is a profound interest in the healthy processes of the self. They tend to think in terms of the personality as a whole. That is a characteristic of American general psychology at the present time. The general trend is to get away from the idea of personality as no more than a sum of its parts, or a bundle of instincts, or an array of conditioned reflexes, or a conglomeration of complexes created by a ruthless 'super-ego'. It is this closer study of the self which is named 'Personalism'.[1]

My own position can be stated in terms of *personalism*. It seems to me absurd that anyone could study psychology or psycho-pathology without a reference to the soul or subject whose experiences are the subject matter of our science. One does not deny 'drives', instinctive tendencies or sentiments, but these can only solicit—they cannot govern. The self has a say in all our experience and probably the final say. After all, it is a self that breaks down, that suffers anxiety-states, that cries to the psychotherapist to relieve it of its guilt and fear and all its other symptoms. We are 'be-souled organisms' as St. Thomas put it. A nervous breakdown, a failure to become adjusted to reality or to become maladjusted to it, is a sign that the self has been unable to unify itself, to bring all its dynamic tendencies under the control of the subject. The problem of all spiritual healing, as it is the special task of psychiatry, is to help the patient to face the situations from which his illness is an escape, or the forgotten experiences to which he reacted badly, or to face his own psychological make-up and his own failure to orient his behaviour tendencies with some meaning to life. It is a self with which we deal and not

---

[1] The last few pages owe a great deal to an article of mine, 'Freudian Psychology' in the *Expository Times*, February 1949.

merely a complex, a character-trend or an external situation. For the exploring of the personality to discover the causes of the failure Freud's methods are unquestionably the best yet conceived. In spite of all the criticisms that can be made of Freud's concepts no one has come anywhere near in his power to analyse the individual soul.

Freudian psychology was not a protest against academic psychology, but a revolt against the strong tendency of the medical profession of his day to assume that mental abnormality of the psycho-neurotic type was due to some somatic cause. Our English medical psychologists are showing at the present time a strong leaning towards somatic treatment of the various types of neurotic and psychotic disease. An excellent description of the various shock treatments given in our mental hospitals is to be found in Dr. A. C. Brown's small volume in *The Thinker's Library*. It has long been a matter of observation that when a neurotic patient was actually ill from some physical disease his or her symptoms tended to disappear for the time being. Why, then, not give the neurotic a physical disease that could be controlled? This is the origin of the modern methods of shock treatment by insulin or metrazol or the electric shocks that cause convulsive fits. It is purely empirical and not based at all on any deeper understanding of neurotic troubles. Were the methods successful then the long analytical treatment could be avoided. But the question is: How successful have these methods been?

Personally I have not come across one patient who has been cured by the new methods, and at the moment I have no less than seven who have undergone the treatment in one form or another. That may be my misfortune. It is just possible that one day there will be found a method by which the disturbing factors will be repressed into the 'deep

unconscious' deeply enough to cause no disturbance either
of the subconscious or conscious mind. It is doubtful
whether the present methods of shock therapy can do this.
In 1939 a Swiss committee of psychiatric experts reported
on their examination of the results of insulin and metrazol
therapy in schizophrenia. They gave six years to their examination. They reported that whereas the duration of the
attack may sometimes be shortened, a real curative effect on
the schizophrenic process from these medications cannot be
established. Certainly some patients improve and leave the
hospital, but that is not unusual in patients who have had
no shock therapy, as Dr. Brill reminds us. It is difficult not
to agree with Dr. Brill when he writes: 'I cannot imagine
how a drug like metrazol or insulin or any other shock
therapy can throw much light on the nature and origin of
schizophrenia except to cover it up'. All the patients I have
seen who have undergone the treatment without cure have
the added symptoms of obsessive thinking about patients
they saw in hospital, plus a deeper pessimism regarding
their condition. Those who use these methods, however, do
not think that they are successful in all cases and, it may
be true, as Dr. A. C. Brown remarks, that 'insulin treatment
is a remarkable advance in the treatment of mental disease'.
There we must leave it.

I have already differentiated between the 'complex', the
'situation neurosis' and the 'character-neurosis'. The first
is the outcome of some traumatic experience which has been
repressed. If the experience can be brought back into consciousness and explored, then integrated with the mature
mind of the patient, the symptoms disappear, as for example in the case of the young woman who had the dream of
two pennies on the grave-stone which brought back the experience with the boy employed on her father's farm. Then

we have the anxiety states which arise through a particular situation or in virtue of some misconception. A good example of this was a young man who was brought to me in a state of acute anxiety. He gave me all sorts of reasons for his anxiety, but a dream led at once to the fact that he had committed a criminal act; the repressed fear of being found out was the root of the trouble. The situation was honestly faced and his anxiety disappeared. The anxiety was entirely due to a particular situation. The 'character-neurosis' is the most deeply seated and is the most difficult to cure, because it involves the self as a whole. It infects almost every act of the self. Dr. Karen Horney has listed ten of these structures and her analysis of them is worth minute study. Dr. Flügel's volume, *Man, Morals and Society,* shows how the prohibitive conscience or super-ego creates many character-structures of a morbid kind. To cure the patient, or even to alleviate the symptoms, these structures have to be changed, and they can only be changed by insight and courage. In the character-neurosis there is a pervading anxiety which tends to disturb all personal relationships. The roots of the structure go back to childhood experiences which were reacted to by anxiety; the experiences were cumulative and because of the anxiety were never integrated. I have already given illustrations of character-neuroses. In these neuroses it is the self that has to be strengthened; it has to be made aware of its weakness, and the will has to be re-enforced.

It was because of this last fact that Dr. McDougall advocated that the psychotherapist should utilise whatever religious faith the patient may have. It should not be used as a substitute for understanding the basic reasons for the trouble, but as an ally to informed perception on the part of the patient of the basic causes of his inability to realise that sense of security which all true religion gives to its devotees.

That brings us to the final method of healing that concerns us here, namely, Spiritual Healing.

Part of the difficulty here is in definition. Can we differentiate between 'Mental Healing' and 'Spiritual Healing'? As far as I understand the writings of spiritual healers the emphasis seems to be laid upon the general spiritual state of the individual. The best school of Spiritual Healing is represented by the Guild of Health, of which the late Rev. Harold Anson was chairman, and who gave us the volume, *Spiritual Healing*. The whole man must be taken into account and not simply the mental processes which manifest themselves in mental disturbance or even in physical disease. In practically all spiritual healing there is the assumption that power can come to the individual from sources outside himself, and that he can by prayer, the sacraments and spiritual devotions increase his capacity to receive that power.

This is the concept of spiritual healing at its best. The whole trend of psychotherapy at the present time is to treat the individual as a whole. In fact, the recent developments in psycho-somatic medicine work on the principle of psycho-organic unity. In the preceding chapters I have emphasised again and again that it is a self that breaks down. That self, I believe, to be a spiritual entity, and its drive for rational and moral unity is the source of the drive for meaning to life and cannot stop short of a spiritual meaning to life, and I should add, cannot stop short of entering into relations with whatever spiritual forces there are in the world.

Nor would one deny the efficacy of prayer, the sacraments or spiritual devotion exercises, in the healing of disease. The late Professor James put the religious view of prayer when he said in his Gifford Lectures: 'Through prayer, religion insists, things which cannot be realised in any other manner come about: energy which but for prayer would be bound is by prayer set free and operates in some part, be it objective or subjective, of the world of facts'. He goes on to quote Frederic W. H. Myers, who had been asked to comment on prayer. 'There exists', says Myers, 'around us a spiritual universe, and that universe is in actual relation with the material. From the spiritual universe comes the energy which maintains the material; the energy which makes the life of each individual spirit. Our spirits are supported by a perpetual indrawal of this energy, and the vigor of that indrawal is perpetually changing, much as the vigor of our absorption of material nutriment changes from hour to hour. . . .

'Plainly we must endeavour to draw in as much spiritual life as possible, and we must place our minds in any attitude which experience shows to be favourable to such indrawal. *Prayer* is the general name for that attitude of open and earnest expectancy . . . . . grace flows in from the infinite spiritual world.'

I am behind no man in my acceptance of the two assumptions of the true spiritual healers. The whole man must be healed, or rather I should say, the *man as a whole*, for as we have seen, the whole individual is not a mere sum of parts. And although I cannot enter here into the metaphysics of the Self, I have no hesitation in saying that I believe that *Self* to be *Spirit*.

Nevertheless, I hold firmly that spiritual healing should always be accompanied, and indeed based on some knowledge of why and how the self has failed to unify its own dynamic elements. Unless some kind of analysis precedes the prayer, the laying on of hands, the anointing with oil, the healer is moving in the dark. That is not to say that spiritual healing even without some kind of analysis is devoid of successes. As long as a patient's symptoms remain mental in the form of anxiety-states or irrational obsessions which the sufferer realises to be irrational, spiritual healing can be effective if the sufferer can be induced to lay hold of God, or to exercise whatever religious faith he may have. There is always the possibility that an interest of an objective kind can be elicited and the individual's thought turned away from himself. That is the technique of Christian Science. The patient's mind is turned outwards away from himself to God. We are all familiar with cases of functional organic disease, or in technical terms, *conversion hysteria*, clearing up after some kind of shock.

The difficulty that I find with spiritual healing as practised in the churches is that there seems to be no attempt to find out what had caused the symptoms of which the sufferer complains. They say the trouble is spiritual, but no real means are taken by which the individual could gain a spiritual insight into his condition and thus prepare the way of healing, or the indrawal of the divine grace.

The problem becomes more complicated when the psychological conflict produces actual physical symptoms, rather than mental ones. Do you think it is easy for a man suffering from peptic ulcer, fibrositis, or a return of tubercular symptoms, or who is failing to respond to treatment to believe that his trouble has anything to do with mental or moral conflicts? Or that the onset of the trouble was a psychological upset or a reaction to a situation in life? And yet, so it may be.

Forgive me if I trouble you with some statistics. Dr. Halliday gives the results of two researches which are relevant here. 'One research was based on a study of insured persons who had been certified as unfit for work by reason of terms indicating non-arthritic rheumatism and who appeared for examination before a medical referee. It showed that at least forty per cent of these were in fact incapacitated not by rheumatism but by psycho-neurotic illness. The other based on a study of fifty patients (mainly from the services) who had been labelled as cases of actual fibrositis showed that in twenty-three of them physical examination was negative, and among the remaining twenty-seven there was a diversity of affections. However, seventy per cent. of all patients were found to suffer from psycho-neurotic illness—twenty-five of them from hysteria and a further ten from states of anxiety and depression.'

Dr. Halliday's comment on the researches is: 'When it is born in mind that perhaps sixty to eighty per cent. of illness labelled rheumatism among the insured population who are on the sick list are examples not of arthritic affections, but of non-arthritic affections, the observations made in these two researches show the "problem of rheumatism" is in no small degree enmeshed with the problem of psycho-neurotic illness'.

Further in the same essay, Dr. Halliday comments: 'As a result of general practitioners seeing their patients in their domestic and social settings most of them come to appreciate that subjective complaints of pain and stiffness seem natural to certain types of persons and also even certain types of life-situation, e.g. bereavement. With increasing experience they realise that therapy in such cases is concerned not only (or indeed not much) with treating the symptoms as with the treating the person whose pseudo-rheumatism seems to be the outward manifestation of inner emotional tensions that have been provoked by disturbing external events or generated through accumulation of internal conflicts. Symptoms of feeling sore and stiff may then represent the patient's deep-seated feelings of being hurt by circumstances and resenting them—in the sense of being sore about things and feeling stiff'. What Dr. Halliday is insisting upon here is that symptoms may be the organic expression of the unconscious.

The quotations are from a volume entitled: *Psychology in General Practice,* and they are from the chapter dealing specially with 'Psycho-somatic Medicine and The Rheumatic Problem'. The chapter immediately preceding it is another chapter on psycho-somatic medicine, and deals with the 'Visceral Neuroses'. Psycho-somatic medicine we may define as that branch of medicine which studies the actual physiological disturbances which originated or were accentuated by a psychological situation or upset. There is here in contrast to hysteria symptoms a definite 'bodily site which is *inferior,* i.e. of *lesser resistance* as a result of an old injury or disease'. A man for one reason or another may have a weak digestion, or a healed tubercular lung; a psychological upset may express itself through lighting up this weakness.

Unfortunately, space will allow me only one illustration; I take it from the pages of *The Lancet* for November, 1946. The article is by Dr. George, resident physician, Mundesley Sanatorium, Norfolk.

Alan, his patient, was a young Irish doctor who developed pulmonary tuberculosis while doing a house physician's job in the South of England. He was a stocky, popular fellow, full of vitality, who rapidly became *persona grata* in the sanatorium. His lesions, however, failed to respond to treatment and he was still on bed rest at the end of six months. 'Everything was done for him, but the disease activity remained stationary.

'Then we crushed his phrenic nerve. It worked like a charm. His diaphragm rose and within a few days his temperature dropped and steadily he became sputum free. And then he awoke one morning with glove-and-stocking paralysis. Being a doctor, he had diagnosed it himself before we could answer his bell and we found him bellowing, "Why have I got conversion hysteria?" He started to sweat and by the end of the week he had shrunk a stone in weight.

'Then one evening in the darkened room he told me his story. He was a Roman Catholic and his fiancée, who was an extremely nice girl, was also a Roman Catholic. But he possessed, as it were, two personalities, a saint who was a devout practising Roman Catholic, and a sinner who wasn't, and they were not on speaking terms. The saint adored his beloved with religious fervour, but the sinner treated her differently. His fiancée was devoted to him, but was ashamed at being forced to enjoy pre-nuptial bliss against her better understanding. So their relationship became degraded in both their eyes and they were pretty miserable though deeply in love with each other. I think it significant that he took a house job in the South of England—just as far from Ireland as he could get.

'Here he became involved with a nurse, developed signs and symptoms of tuberculosis (with confessed relief) and sped back to his mother and fiancée. He was not too easy there and he again elected to cross large tracts of land and water to Mundesley, where he was happy. And now when he shows signs of getting better he himself gets sick in spirit. It seemed obvious that he was not yet ready to re-enter the world from which tuberculosis had afforded him an escape. He had then to realise that saint and sinner had to be reconciled—the self must have wholeness. Once he realised that, he sent for his fiancée, confessed everything, was forgiven, and made a rapid and uninterrupted recovery.'

Dr. George gives many other examples of the disease giving an opportunity to patients to escape some of life's difficult situations and contradictions. Other writings could have given me illustrations, and I have not a few I could have taken from my own note-book. I have chosen this one because it illustrates what is meant by a psychological upset influencing actual physical disease without being the actual cause of it. I have also selected the case because it is just the kind of case that might have been cured at Lourdes, as the atmosphere is such as would be likely to induce the confession which was the turning point in the doctor's recovery.

Psycho-somatic medicine is based on the assumption of the unity between the body and the mind—the mind affects the body and the body affects the mind. Probably there is no mental distress which does not cause some disturbance of physiological functioning. Certainly there are few psychological breakdowns which do not show some disturbance of digestion or sleep. One can say that there is a mental factor in all disease—anxiety or worry of some kind. That the mind affects the body is the assumption throughout the whole history of medicine, and religion and medicine have been connected since the days of Æsculapius. It would be interesting to digress and say something of the methods of spiritual healing in the early temples, and the evidence of the success attained. As, however, there are volumes dealing with the history of spiritual and faith-healing available we must forgo the digression. Enough to say that in the earliest civilisations the connection between the mind or soul and disease was recognised. Dr. Dearmer, in his *Body and Soul,* gives an excellent account of Faith-Healing from the second century to quite recent times, a whole chapter is given to the reported cures at Lourdes.

Turning to the New Testament, we find that our Lord recognised this union of body and mind, and He assumed a connection between the moral and spiritual state and the diseases He cured. To the paralytic He gave absolution before He said 'Take up thy bed and walk'; 'See that you sin no more lest a worse thing befall thee' was His parting word to the man healed at the Pool of Bethesda. 'Thy faith has saved thee' He said to the woman who touched His garment. 'Dost thou believe?' He asked the father of the epileptic boy. Unquestionably our Lord performed acts of spiritual healing. Christ's method was not always the same. He mixed clay and spittle and anointed the eyes of one blind man. In regard to the epileptic boy's cure He said 'This kind can come forth by nothing, but by prayer and fasting.' As a rule His method was direct suggestion. He must have believed that the body could be affected through the mind, and He was aware that repressed sin could affect the body and cause these functional paralyses and contractures which He cured. Unconfessed sin can affect the body as we have seen in the case of the Roman Catholic doctor, and the realisation of the sin, repentance and confession with the fiancée's forgiveness was followed by rapid healing of his bodily disease.

There is another thing we should keep in mind. Doctors are not unfamiliar with cases of disease of an organic kind clearing up for no known reason. In psycho-neurotic trouble this spontaneous clearing up of paralyses, hysterical symptoms, anxiety and depression states and even stammer is by no means uncommon. There are numbers of people who have suffered from various neurotic symptoms,

I

especially phobias, and who were never able to consult anyone about their troubles and who have become completely
free. We can only surmise that the repressed cause of the
trouble found some outlet agreeable to the conscious mind,
or that the psychological conditions behind the trouble
were altered sufficiently to relieve the mind of its burden
of symptoms.

These examples I have given show, I think, that the
assumption of psycho-somatic unity is a legitimate hypothesis; and I think that it is here that we may look for an
explanation of the effectiveness of spiritual healing. From
ancient times prayer, faith and the laying on of hands have
been, to say the least, coincident with healing. In the cases
treated by psychotherapy the cure has been effected by a
subjective change in the individual. I have treated many
cases where the symptoms were markedly physical. Here
is a married woman who was sent with functional disturbance of the heart. She was married just before the late war
to a conscientious objector. She had no children and consequently was compelled to find a job. Naturally she took,
or rather thought she took, her husband's views of war. I
quickly found from her dreams that she was back with
old boy friends who had joined up. Yet there was nothing
in the woman that really wanted to renew friendship with
these old boy friends; she undoubtedly preferred her husband. The dreams gave me the clue to the fact that she did
not really agree with her husband's conscientious objections
to war, and she would have preferred that he had joined
up. That was verified as I got down to the root of the disturbance. When she went to apply for a job she was invariably asked what her husband was doing; the same
question was asked by those who worked with her in the
office. She dreaded what they would think if she told them

that he was a conscientious objector. She came to dread the question being asked; her heart would start to thump; the same symptom would appear when she walked up the avenue where she lived, and she imagined that the people whose husbands or sons were at the war despised both her and her husband. She tried changing her job; but the same question was asked. Finally she had to give up work altogether; and the disturbance of the heart gave her the escape she wanted from all her questioners. She improved immediately she faced the whole question. Curiously enough she had a recurrence of the trouble when there came to live next door to her one who knew all about her husband's conscientious objection and that he went on to the land during the war. Naturally had there not been a pre-disposition to fear criticism and disapproval she would have taken a different reaction to what people might think of her husband, but the immediate cause of the trouble was as I have stated. Her cure was due to a subjective change.

Here is another patient whose symptoms were markedly physical. She was sent with a gross tremor which interfered with the co-ordinated action of both arms and hands. Only with very great difficulty could she raise a tumbler or cup to her lips, and to button her coat was a task indeed. The trouble originated when her father, a devout practising Roman Catholic, gave her a devotional book in which there was a sentence: 'There are parts of the body which should only be touched for purposes of cleanliness'. At once she began to tremble. She had been indulging in a form of masturbation which apparently she had never realised until she read that sentence about 'mortal sin'. The whole tendency to the act was repressed and the tremor increased. At the end of the first interview she was able to do what she had not done for months, namely, take a glass of water comfortably to her lips and drink it without the slightest tremor. I sent her to her confessor, who sent her back for one more interview and with some questions he wanted me to answer.

I remember a doctor friend of mine being very distressed because his daughter had got infantile paralysis. She was one of the brightest children I ever knew. All that one could do in a case like that was to help the girl to adjust herself to the condition, and to help her to live her life in spite of her lameness. That she did, and she has led as nearly a normal life as her disability would allow her. She can swim, she has no inferiority complex, and is a happy woman now.

I do not believe that any kind of spiritual or faith-healing could have done anything but increase hope that could never be fulfilled, and then leave her disappointed and embittered.

On the other hand, take a patient of mine who developed a contracture of muscles in his leg. I suspected it was psychological. As a precaution he was sent to the orthopædic surgeon, who put his leg in plaster for three months without result; for another three months the leg was put in plaster and again without beneficial effects. I then analysed and found that the condition was due to the drawing up of his leg as a defence reaction against unpleasant stimuli. He was taught to react to the stimuli in a normal way, and today he will walk without difficulty for miles.

We have seen in the case of the Irish doctor how unconfessed sin may have effects in physical disease. He experienced relief when his symptoms meant that he could give up his job in the hospital and escape his temptations; I do not think that he was altogether ignorant that some connection existed between his failure to respond to treatment and his moral lapses, in other words, between his illness and his spiritual condition. I believe there are many who do sense a link between their mental or physical condition and their way of life, and when they go for spiritual healing keep their spiritual condition in the focus of their mind. It is in such people that prayer, faith and spiritual healing have their greatest effects. I mentioned the case of the man of sixty-five who fell ill and whose symptoms were depression and a disturbance of the alimentary functions. Next to his last visit he said to me: 'You know I am beginning to feel that I need a purpose in life, to be of service to somebody'. There at the back of this man's mind there must have been the feeling that what was wrong with him was a lack of spiritual meaning to life and a lack of spiritual resources.

On the other hand, when we get a patient who is altogether pre-occupied with his symptoms, who is willing to pray for their removal, but has repressed the causes of them, spiritual healing in my opinion is in vain. Even God should not be asked to remove effects while the causes remain unaltered. Prayer and faith or spiritual acts such as the anointing with oil or the laying on of hands when directed to symptoms alone without any adequate attempt to understand why the symptoms are there at all is never effective. The symptoms are defence reactions against offending tendencies. Lift the symptoms without replacing control of offending tendencies by conscious agencies and the state of that patient will be worse than at first. Did not our Lord warn against the casting out of the devil without replacing him by other and higher interests? Did He not warn those whom He cured and forgave against sinning again—that is to say, taking advantage of their freedom from anxiety or physical symptoms to indulge again in the behaviour which was the root of their trouble? That is one of the dangers of physical therapies and why there are many relapses; the patient may become for a time free from his symptoms, but as he has not had any insight into the causes of these symptoms he indulges behaviour-tendencies to which his symptoms were defence reactions, and he then cracks again badly. Neither prayer nor faith should be asked to do the work of magic. Faith, we should remember, is not a calculus of probabilities, nor is it believing in propositions whose grounds are inaccessible to logic; faith is an encounter with God; and we cannot encounter God with a host of unacknowledged character-structures or offending behaviour-tendencies and expect to be healed. Where the inner condition which is affecting the mind or body and causing symptoms is known, and that inner condition brought to God in prayer, and His help sought in faith, then spiritual healing results. For spiritual healing to be effective the drive for spiritual wholeness must be greater than the mere fear of the symptoms and their results. Even God cannot divorce effects from causes; He cannot remove anxiety from a man or woman whose soul is threatened by reprehensible emotions or behaviour tendencies, or character-structures which have been re-pressed. These tendencies must be brought to conscious-ness. As a rule, such patients cannot pray. In all of them I have found a moral unwillingness to renounce the offend-ing tendencies, and often the disguised wish to seek the pleasure without the guilt. On the other hand, some of them cannot pray because as a penalty for those unrepented tendencies they punish themselves by banishing God, and the felt alienation from Him can be a severe form of self-punishment.

A type of patient which I believe spiritual healing can help effectively is one mentioned by Dr. Halliday who really suffers because external circumstances have been too much for him or her. They do not fear prohibited tendencies but they shrink from hard situations. The individual may be afraid to acknowledge to himself as well as to others how he fears certain conditions of life. Often the fear has just to be acknowledged for the individual to take a new reaction to whatever circumstances have created his self-pity, self-condemnation or physical symptoms, and consequently for the symptoms to disperse. Often symptoms are produced, as we have seen, to get sympathy or attention. If this is acknowledged, faith, prayer or Christian Science can be effective. Dr. Halliday instances the rheumatism of the poet Coleridge, whose biographer tells us that he showed great discretion in his choice of the households in which to fall ill! He also gives the case of a Salvation Army officer who consulted him for what the doctor diagnosed as false appendicitis; he suggested to the officer that there was no organic basis of the trouble, but instead of the patient being relieved that there was nothing really dangerous in his condition, he became very huffy. Two days later he wrote the doctor to tell him that the night following his interview, 'The Lord had cured him'!

I believe that research should be made as to the type of person who can be relieved and helped by spiritual healing. The mere blind laying on of hands, or uninformed prayers for a return to health without any attempt to know the causes of the mental distress or the hysterical symptoms is spiritually unhealthy. It is acting like a surgeon who just plunges his knife into a human body with no idea what to look for or where his knife is needed. Where the individual has not lost entirely his sense of God, his belief in prayer, or whose faith still gives an active flicker, all those should be utilised as Dr. McDougall contended, to help the individual to realise that there is no inner condition of his soul with which God cannot help him to deal in such a way as to make him 'more than conqueror'. Now that medicine is laying bare a new field of causal factors in psycho-somatic medicine, one has an explanation of the undoubted cures which spiritual healing, Christian Science or Lourdes can justly claim. Although I have looked long and earnestly for some case of spiritual healing or faith-healing of a disease whose cause was purely physical in origin and not correlated with any psychological disturbance, I have never been fortunate enough to see one. One hears of them at second hand. Dr. Somerville[1] mentions two remarkable cases which came under his own observation; one was a tubercular case, and one with cancer in the cheek so bad that the doctor refused to operate. In the tubercular case the patient was anxious to give his life in service to God; the removal of his disease was asked for by a group of praying people, and the man was healed. In the second case prayer was continually offered by the church, and the man was healed. One must not, however, forget how many people have been as earnestly prayed for and nothing has happened. Whatever the explanation of these two cases may be, Dr. Somerville is not likely to substitute prayer for his surgeon's knife; he neglects neither in practice.

That prayer and faith have psychotherapeutic value I have proved again and again. There is no greater preventative of neurotic trouble, and perhaps no greater help to a cure than confessional prayer. It is the indiscriminate resort to faith, prayer and laying-on of hands that I would ask you to deprecate. Let all the religious helps be used,

[1] 'After Everest.'

but let them be used along with all our knowledge of disease both physical and mental; but they must not be used as substitutes for the means open to our hands of restoring both the mind and the body. Spiritual healing is based upon the demand to heal the whole man, body and soul. That is the same demand as psycho-somatic medicine makes, and every good psychotherapist treats the man and not his symptoms. With a deeper understanding of the effects on his health of the individual's spiritual outlook on life, medicine and religion will be drawn closer together.

I cannot define my own position better than in the words of Dr. Wm. Brown, who is no enemy of spiritual healing, and whose psychological work and studies are always linked with philosophy. In his latest volume he writes: 'The process of spiritual healing is a process of arousing faith, the faith-state, and that faith-state may have different degrees of rationality, which is the same thing as saying that it may range over a smaller or larger area of the self, and if it is limited to a small part of the self, it may mislead the individual instead of helping him. One reason why some of us are very doubtful of the wisdom of spiritual healing services is that for many who attend such services it is an appeal to superficial emotion and to primitive credulity. There is a tendency to intensify that hysterical condition of mind from which many patients are already suffering. In some cases there may be a disappearance of hysterical symptoms and an apparent cure, but only at the expense of replacement by another symptom— namely, reliance on quasi-miraculous possibility, the expectation of getting something for nothing, as it were, of getting direct gifts without full appreciation of corresponding demands upon personality'.[1]

[1] 'Personality and Religion,' p. 143 f.

Counseling

This is another method of therapy which demands more than a passing word. The very spelling of the word shows it comes from America, to which country we owe, as we have seen, real advance of psycho-analytical theory.

Here the advance is not so much on theory as in therapy, and it indicates a much wider field for mental therapy than any other theory. There is theory underlying its method of treatment, but there is nothing new in that direction. So far as theory is concerned, it lays emphasis on releasing the rigid emotionalized attitudes of those who are finding it difficult to become adjusted to their immediate circumstances; then, the counsellor does not attempt to direct the interview but to give significant expression to every emotional attitude as it comes to the surface.

The spread of this type of therapy in America and New Zealand is really remarkable. It is not always realised by the public that there are a great many more people needing psychological help than come to any doctor's or psychiatrist's consulting rooms. This new movement has given an opportunity for those who have not actually broken down or been unable to do their work to come and get help through which they become more adjusted to life in all its phases.

How widespread the movement has become can be judged by the fact that there is scarcely a University which has not its counsellor to whom a student can go with his difficulties. What we in England would call a 'welfare officer' is there a counsellor able to give needed counsel in all difficulties not actually demanding the skilled psychiatrist. Counseling is not a matter merely of giving advice; it is a method of therapy and is now entering into competition with other methods of mental healing. It is being raised to a fine art by the scientific application of psychological principles. Although practised by some medical practitioners, it is largely in the hands of non-medical men and women. The services of the counsellor can be had at the famous Rochester (New York) Guidance Centre, and in the well-known Judge Baker Guidance Centre. What we call 'Marriage Guidance Councils' have their analogue in America, and here counseling has been very successful. Social workers are now going far beyond the usual monetary help, or advising about employment or putting the family in touch with a doctor when that is needed; they are also offering counseling help and thus enabling their clients to meet some of the problems which underlie their need of aid at all.

Naturally, counseling has been applied to Pastoral work of the ministry, and a really important volume has been written by Seward Hiltner: *Pastoral Counseling*. Other well-known names come to mind, such as Roy Burkhart, and John Sutherland Bonnell, whose *Pastoral Psychiatry* gives 'discerning counsel for those who would make their pastoral service no mere routine, but a vital ministry to needy personalities'.

That indeed is the essential aim of all counseling—to give help to needy personalities. It does this by releasing through expression the emotionalized attitudes which so often lie behind unadjusted and maladjusted personalities. This is done through the interview in which the client is able to talk up and hence to talk out all his difficulties. The task of the counsellor is non-directive; in so far as he is handling the interview in a scientific manner he will be helping the client to write his own prescription, in other words he will help clients to see and help themselves.

No one has done more to put counseling on a scientific basis than Professor Carl R. Rogers of Chicago University, who was formerly director of the Rochester Guidance Centre. His latest volume, *Counseling and Psychotherapy*, will give far more insight into this method of helping 'needy personalities' to become adjusted to life in all its phases than any other volume I know. He deals with the type of person who is likely to benefit from counseling; he also shows how the emotionalized attitudes become released through expression, and there is a very fine chapter on insight which, after all, is the real cure for any mental failure of adjustment. He illustrates all he writes by extracts from the phonographically recorded interviews with clients. A whole series of eight interviews is recorded, and one can watch for oneself the change taking place in the clients' attitudes. Another volume in which Professor Rogers has a part is a *Case-book of Non-Directive Counseling* by William U. Snyder. Here five cases are given from phonographic records of interviews along with the comments both on the progress made by the client in each interview and on the handling of the interview by the Counsellor. I personally gained a great deal of benefit from both these volumes; and also from the volume by Seward Hiltner on *Pastoral Counseling*.

The significance of the movement lies in this: it is the sign that we are leaving behind us the stage when the sole interest was in diagnosis, or at least the main interest. Most of us have been interested in analysis and diagnosis more than we have been interested in the persons analysed. Now the emphasis is being placed upon therapy and cure. The interest of the counsellor is in the processes by which the individual can be helped to re-adjust himself to life. The adjustment of the individual is the vital thing, not our theories.

The movement is all to the good. As I have said, there are numbers of people who need help who are not bad enough to need the psychiatrist, and yet who have little peace of mind and who are failing to make the best of their opportunities. It is this great multitude to whom counseling will be a real benefactor; it helps and helps quickly; and I am perfectly sure it has saved many from falling into a severe neurosis.

On the other hand, I am inclined to think that it would not be very helpful in cases where repression is deep, or in conversion hysteria cases, or in any of the cases where difficulties are deeply hidden from consciousness. In most of the counseling cases I have read the difficulties were conscious or rather nearly so, and it was not difficult with the skilled help of the counsellor to make them perfectly conscious, so conscious that the client really suggested his own cure.

Although the successful counsellor does not do much interpretation in the interview, he needs must know what the interpretation is. That means that he needs not less knowledge of psychology, normal and abnormal, but more if he is to guide the interview into fruitful channels. In the hands of men like Rogers and Snyder one can see how successful the non-directive interview can become. I learned much from their handling of the interview and I feel sure that this method of treatment has a great future. On the other hand, in the hands of the unskilful this method will simply waste the time of client and would-be counsellor. Clients can talk not to reveal the roots of their difficulties but to hide them! I like the whole movement also because it is not merely an attempt to heal minds, but also to care for souls. Counseling is what will be demanded from every social worker, personnel chief, welfare officers, and marriage guidance counsellors. It is certainly here the pastor will find out how to help his people.

RELIGION AND NERVOUS DISORDERS

IT will not be out of place if in the introduction to the final
lecture I draw your attention to the fact that for the great
mass of people, and indeed for many medical psychologists, psychology is synonymous with Psycho-analysis or
McDougall's Instinctive psychology. This has been a dis-
advantage to psychological science because both these
psychologies give an inadequate analysis of the springs of
behaviour as well as of personality itself. The popular
mind has taken practically all it knows about psychology
from popular expositions of Freudian concepts. The terms
'complex' and 'repression' caught hold of the imagination
and along with the term 'sexuality' were supposed to
explain all sorts of behaviour. Every deviation from the
normal was supposed to be due to a complex, and the shy,
restrained individual was thought to be suffering from
repression. As I have already noted in the previous lecture,
Freud, although he built up a rather impressive psychology,
strong enough to attract the attention of psychologists,
really made his finest contribution in the sphere of psychiatry more than in general psychology. There are large
tracts of psychology which Freud never touched at all.
McDougall more than any other psychologist, at least in
this country, was responsible for the widespread popularity
of the idea that all behaviour was due to the urge of instincts. The theory lent itself to easy explanations of both
normal and abnormal behaviour, and with his idea (which
was first mooted by Shand) that our instincts became

organised within sentiments, character was also explained. The theory is simple to understand : our attention is attracted to something novel because we have a curiosity instinct; the sexes are attracted to each other by the sexual instinct; we become angry when thwarted because we have a pugnacious instinct; we love to show off because we have a self-display instinct. These instincts became organised into sentiments and thus we had character. The emotions which McDougall, in his first exposition, thought were integral elements of instinct, were capable of being compounded and we got all the complex emotions, such as Awe and Reverence. It was all very simple and very interesting in comparison with the older psychology. There was one unfortunate result, however. No two psychologists gave us the same catalogue of instincts! This rather confused matters; and the confusion was not lessened by the capacity of journalists to invent an instinct for every form of behaviour not accounted for in the usual catalogue. An Archdeacon of the Church of England spoke the other day of his 'instinct for pacificism'; theologians began to speak of a 'religious instinct', dramatic critics of a 'histrionic instinct', reviewers of novels spoke of writers having an instinct for a 'dramatic situation'. McDougall in his later books modified his view of instinct and spoke of propensities to this or that kind of behaviour. He believed that he was helping to break down the old 'faculty' view of behaviour; and to some extent he did help us to get away from the idea of a 'faculty of memory', of 'thought', of 'imagination', etc. But a great deal of his psychology simply substituted 'instinct' for 'faculty'. He had no real doctrine of reason or of the self. Reason to him, as to Hume, had no initiative of its own; its function was to present to consciousness the means by which the instincts could be satisfied. Character was just the sum of the sentiments, and there was no real explanation as to why we should have one set of sentiments rather than another. Truly, like animals, we were pushed from behind. Conscience was no more than the voice of the herd, and the fear or approval of the herd decided our moral leanings. His theory kept intact the doctrine of continuity and thus was scientific, but it did nothing to explain our fundamental differences from the animal.

Contemporaneous with Freud and McDougall a great deal of psychological experiment and thought were being carried on in many fields. These schools of psychology had their interest concentrated almost wholly on normal mental processes, and it was they rather than the Freudians or Instinctivists who finally created the separation of psychology from philosophy and laid the foundations of modern psychology.

It is impossible here even to mention the various contributions of the schools to the psychology of education, industry, vocation, ethics. Nor can we go deeply into the psychology of religious experience. There is one school, however, which helps us immensely to understand how the mind is able creatively to go beyond the concepts which can be inferred from experience; while there is another school which has attempted to throw light on the problem of the self or subject of experience. What these schools teach is relevant to what I wish to say on religion and nervous disorders. First of all are the advances in our knowledge of intelligence and how it works. I believe that Spearman's doctrine of 'noe-genesis' is a true answer to the Freudian contention that religion is a projection, although not the only answer. The relevant part of Spearman's work is to be found in his principle of correlated

K

eductions. When we have got a known item of experience with a known relation, we spontaneously tend to educe a correlated item. In other words, there is natural tendency for the mind to transcend its experience and to have ideas that not only go beyond experience but of objects which we could not experience through the senses. Such ideas are Eternity, Immortality and Perfection. Then we have the attributes of God. No one can experience the omniscience or omnipotence of God, yet they are objects of thought not in virtue of projection or mediated inference, but in virtue of the creative tendency of the mind to go beyond experience. I mention this in passing, as many find Freud's projection theory difficult to answer. Psychologically there are 'several ways of accounting for the occurrence in knowledge of concepts or notions, some of which do not take us beyond the range of empirical experience, while others enable us to transcend it'.[1] It is doubtful if theologians have made as much use of Spearman's theories as might have been done.

The school most relevant to our position is the 'Personality School'. All schools have the problem of personality as their ultimate aim, but this latest school concentrates entirely almost on the study of personality as a whole. It is a comparatively young school. They acknowledge that much knowledge has accrued from the study and listing of various personality-traits, and from the fact that the laboratory has been able to assess the strength of will, depth of interest and temperamental influences. Nevertheless, their interest is not so much on the traits as on the principle that integrates the whole into a personality.

[1] 'The Psychological Approach to Reality', by Francis Aveling, p. 71.

Naturally much attention has been given to the definition of personality. Here is the definition given by Professor Gordon W. Allport, one of the leaders of the
school in America: 'Personality is the dynamic organiza-
tion within the individual of those psycho-physical systems
that determine the unique adjustments to his environment'.[1] The emphasis is laid upon 'unique'. They stress
individuality; and they criticise the other schools of experimental psychology because they generalise as if there was
such a thing as 'mind in general', an 'individual in general',
whereas the individual is unique. They complain that the
tendency of the experimental schools is to scatter the
attention upon details of behaviour and to forget that
personality is a whole, and that the integrating factor of
organisation must not be forgotten. Even the study of
intelligence is apt to abstract intelligence from the intelligent individual. That we owe much to the study of single
attributes no one will deny. Probably there is no other way
in which a score can be given for single attributes or
character-traits; but when one has given a score for intelligence, rote memory, retentivity, perseverance, etc., the
mere sum of these scores, as Allport like the Gestalt
school reminds us, does not give personality.

One curious thing about this school is that it avoids
the metaphysical implications. But the fundamental question for the psycho-therapist, as well as for the preacher
and social worker is: has the individual, the integrating
principle of personality, a say in what shall be integrated?
If personality is something more than the sum of its parts,
what is the something more? The school raises great hopes;
but it is doubtful whether it will be the fulfilment of
Professor James's prophecy that one day psychology would

[1] 'Personality: A Psychological Interpretation,' p. 48.

produce its Galileo or Lavoisier who would also be a metaphysician.[1]

It will be obvious that my own psychology is 'Personalist'. To me the integrating principle of the dynamic organisation is the Self or Subject with its own dynamic tendency towards a self-conscious harmonious individual or whole. And I believe that the more self-conscious the tendency becomes, the greater say the self has in determining its adjustments and what will be integrated into the personality. To the degree that the individual consciously or unconsciously attempts to integrate what is inconsistent with a moral and spiritual whole to that degree he fails to realise a unified personality or breaks down.

Now it would be agreed by all psychologists that religious experience has a determining effect on the integration of the self. Not that psychologists necessarily accept the objectivity of religious beliefs. We have already seen that Freud contended that God is the projected need of the Father. James, on the other hand, believed there was a 'something there', and the feeling of that 'something there' was a moment in the religious experience and not simply an inference. Just as our experience of objectivity and externality is a moment in our sense experience of phenomena in the external world. We don't infer from our sense experience that there is a table or chair there, nor do we project the table or chair; on the contrary, the objectivity and the externality of the table and chair are part of the sense experience. Otto[2] attempted to describe the 'something there' as the 'numen' whose presence we experience through the activity of the numinous disposition.

[1] The preceding pages owe much to an article of mine in *Expository Times*, March, 1949: 'After Freud.'

[2] 'The idea of The Holy.'

It would take us too far to go into a critical estimate of those positions. But what we can say with confidence is that we can only respond or experience a situation if we have something to respond with. The very fact that we respond to the super sensuous is proof that we are endowed with some capacity that gives meaning to the super-sensuous experience. That does not imply that we have a 'religious instinct'. Such a concept reduces religion to a biological need for its explanation; whereas religion, like ethics, logic and art must go beyond biological needs for their explanation. Animals have biological needs, but they have no religious experience.[1] The individual's personality-need to realise himself as a self-conscious, spiritual whole with its drive for rational and moral unity, must, we believe, be invoked here. Given that the *telos* in man is the image of God striving to realise itself, to grow into the stature of Christ, and we have the real roots of religious experience. The dynamic image of God, the *telos* in man, is that which responds to the confrontation of God. Were there nothing in our nature that could respond to the supersensuous, to God, to the moral ideal, it would be psychologically impossible to explain man's interest and pre-occupation with religion. The very relish with which a Hume or Freud set out to undermine the objectivity of religious experience, shows, at its least, that they are not indifferent to it, and at its most, that it may be an over-compensation for the repressed drive for that rational unity which cannot stop short of God, the very source of the unity and rationality of the universe which all thinkers seek.

One could go further here were one writing specifically on the psychology of religious experience. Granted that

[1] Cf. 'Revelation and Reason,' Brünner, p. 259.

we can only respond to a situation if we have something to respond with, does it follow that a need implies and indeed involves the object to which we can respond and the object that satisfies the need? Hunger not merely implies food, but involves it; sex implies a mate; intelligence implies objects of knowledge. Every need, be it biological or personal, implies the objects that can satisfy. If man has a numinous disposition that involves a *numen,* just as structure involves function in biology. As Bosanquet[1] has put it: 'But *in rerum natura* an instinct implies its object; and if you find a special emotional impulse, such as that of worship and religion, which pervades all sorts of particular experiences, but maintains its unique suggestion and demand throughout them all, you can hardly help recognising the object of this emotion as at least some peculiar feature of the world'. Religion, we must remember, is not merely an idea of God but an experience of God. Alas! the content of the idea of God is not given but acquired and has a determining effect on the experience of God.

But I must not allow myself to get too entangled in philosophy. I must stick to empirical fact. If we accept Spearman's theory of correlated educts, then the concept of God, His attributes and much else that transcends experience are yet empirically produced not by mediate inference, but by the natural creativity of the mind. And if we accept the doctrine of the *telos* of man as the image of God, then the very *nisus* of his personality is towards God and the realisation of that image in the self-conscious harmonious whole.

The interest in religion in these lectures lies in the fact that it plays such a large part in the nervous disorders of

[1] 'Contemporary Philosophy,' p. 68.

tion. We can see the effects of such a religion best in the neurotic character-trends it produces. Invariably those people whose religion is a Religion of Law suffer from what Karen Horney calls The Neurotic Character-Trend to Restrict their Life within Narrow Limits. The moral life becomes hedged in by all sorts of restrictions, and the sense of guilt can be excited by the most trivial indulgence, such as buying a newspaper on Sunday, a glass of wine, attendance at a theatre or any sensual pleasure. The natural drives of the personality come into conflict with these unhealthy prohibitions and restrictions and a severe neurosis may result with symptoms of guilt, hostility to God for which deeper guilt is incurred. Fortunately most people can impose a good deal of morbid restrictions upon themselves without becoming pathological, but if the pathological stage is reached, then the neurosis can be very severe. When we impose restrictions upon ourselves on truly moral grounds we may find them irksome, but they cause no morbid symptoms. Those with the neurotic restriction character-trend are not governed by moral considerations at all; they are the victims of repressed fear of breaking a law which has come to act like a taboo. If they go beyond their self-imposed restriction by some simple indulgence, or if by some oversight they have forgotten to do something their code demands, such as to read their morning passage of Scripture, they suffer guilty feelings as if they had committed a great sin. These are the people who hedge themselves round with all sorts of what they sometimes call 'Whims'; one individual had to cross the square in her township at one particular point; she must not go into a teashop for tea; for twenty-five years she felt it would be a sin to go to a hairdresser. The more severe cases have a good deal of their day taken up by all kinds of ritual acts; this, that and the other thing must be placed in a certain way, the toes of the shoes of one patient had to point towards the door when she laid them aside for the night; the table-cloth had to be folded from the left side, and at table she could hand things to others only with her left hand. From morning to night some of these people are consciously trying to avoid doing anything or even hearing anything that could incur guilt. One woman was compelled to put on the wireless and yet was afraid all the time that she might hear something that would make her feel guilty.

In a previous lecture I mentioned the neurotic structure of Perfectionism. Here the vital characteristic is the neurotic striving to be above temptation, unassailable by it. To the undiscriminating, such people might be striving to grow in grace. As a matter of psychological fact it is a compulsive tendency and is an over-compensation for a basal sense of moral insecurity. An extreme case I had was a girl who was telling herself all day that she was not a bad girl. These people are the very opposite of the man who said: 'There, but for the grace of God go I', when he saw a prisoner being taken for execution. To a large extent this was the religion of St. Paul before his conversion—'as, touching the righteousness of the law, blameless'. No one doubts the basic sense of insecurity in Paul before his experience on the Damascus Road; and as an over-compensation he must not only keep the law, but he must surpass others; he was a Hebrew of the Hebrews, as touching the law a Pharisee, a member of the strictest sect. It was characteristic of the Pharisees to look down on others; they had a feeling of superiority because of their perfect obedience to the law. That characteristic can be seen in all perfectionists. It was very characteristic of the members of the Oxford Group Movement in its early days with their stress upon absolute purity, honesty, etc. One has just to probe a little into the mind of the perfectionists to find that underneath there is a tremendous fear of finding that they are weak and full of faults. When the perfectionist does break down, the sense of guilt is overpowering.

What is the psychological effect of this type of religion? As we have said, it re-enforces the prohibitive conscience and thus prevents the individual from attaining to a mature religion. The relationship between the individual and God remains juridical. The victim of it tends to project the severity of his own infantile conscience both upon the law and upon God. Law should be a guide post, not a series of barriers. 'Thy statutes have become my song in the house of my pilgrimage' sings the Psalmist. Here is true insight into the relation of law to religious experience. The 'statutes' are not barriers; their function is to give guidance and insight into moral situations. That as we have seen is what the mature conscience gives, and always characterises the mature adult with a mature religious experience.

We often see this kind of projection upon the earthly parent. It is not uncommon for patients to describe their father as tyrannical and repressive when he was really nothing of the kind. The child and adolescent will project upon the parent the threatenings of his own prohibitive conscience. This invariably keeps the child or adolescent from entering into free and affectionate relations with the parent.

Apart from all this, or rather in addition to it, the religion of law cuts across the need for affection—the need to love and to be loved. A juridical religion simply cannot be assimilated and lies over against the personality and its behaviour-tendencies as a continuous threat. Such a religion tends to excite a premature sense of guilt. At its best this type of religion can produce an unhappy holiness as can be seen in those persons who, without breaking down, develop one or other, perhaps both of the character-structures of restriction or perfectionism. At its worst it produces the neuroses in which compulsive hand-washing, ritual acts, a multitude of moral scruples which must be meticulously observed under fierce threats from within, are symptoms. To refuse to comply with one of those 'musts' creates unbearable anxiety tension. Here is one young girl of twelve years of age who *must* go to school without breakfast; she must kneel on the doormat and kiss it before she goes out anywhere; she must kiss every piece of furniture in the bedroom before she goes to bed.

The *Religion of Authority* is another type which can cause a great deal of neuroticism. Here submission to authority is reckoned as equivalent to faith. Dogmas must be believed on authority; God must be submitted to.

Now we know that submission unless motivated by insight invariably sets up hostility in the unconscious. It is really astonishing the amount of active hostility to God one hears from patients whose unconscious attitude to religion is motivated by submission. The conflict in these patients is that between the natural drive for individuation and freedom and the unhealthy unconscious wish to be under authority. They fear freedom; they fear making decisions on their own initiative, and yet they hate authority. They become psychologically dependent on others, and yet hostile to the very people on whom they are dependent. They hate the chains with which they have bound themselves. Someone has to tell them what to do and they do it, but inwardly they rebel because their acts are not their own.

Naturally their religion is determined by the same character-structure. They comply with what they believe to be God's commands, but underneath they are rebels. The unconscious conflict between the drive of natural impulses, as well as the natural drive for freedom from unwholesome restraints, and the compulsive tendency to submit may reach such a tension that there is a breakdown. In these patients the guilt feelings become intense, and they become intensified by compulsive tendencies to take God's name in vain, or to utter obscene words or extreme forms of negativism as though they were refusing to submit. All of them suffer from some degree of what I should call melancholic anxiety, and indeed the melancholic anxiety may be the chief symptom.

There may be, however, no breakdown. If the tendency to rebel is stronger than the compulsive tendency you get the extreme leftist whose rebellious tendency may express itself in left wing politics, in which religion is scorned; or it may express itself in the religious field in which the individual becomes a restless propagandist against religion. The submissive tendency, nevertheless, has its say; it can express itself in a fanatical submission to a political creed, or a political leader as in communism; and in many of the anti-religious propagandists there will be found a strict morality and integrity. If, on the other hand, the submissive tendency has the upper hand, the individual becomes a 'Yes' man with an insipid personality with servility as one of its traits. There is no growth of the personality; there is a childish relationship to God. All is accepted as coming from an inscrutable divine providence, much as a child accepts and submits to the irritable demands and arbitrary actions of the parents.

Another type of personality is due to the religion of authority, namely, the Fundamentalist. The submissive tendency is strong enough to force an absolute acceptance of the Scriptures; not one jot or tittle must be questioned. The rebel tendency is kept in check by absolute intellectual obedience to the Word. Those in whom the rebellious tendency cannot be absolutely repressed are oppressed by doubts, fears and moral scruples.

The psychological objections to this religion of authority are that it cuts across the personality-need for rational and moral unity as well as the drive for individuation and psychological independence. My own impression after reading Miss Petre's *My Way of Faith* is that all her scruples, or *spiritual vermin* as she calls them, were produced by this conflict between the drive for rational unity and the necessity to believe what she was taught by the Church. Fortunately for her the balance was held by her spontaneous love of the Church and its ritual and services. In virtue of this 'Piety' as she terms this spontaneous love of the Church she was able to express much that was in sympathy with the modernist school in the Roman Church without making an absolute break in her allegiance to the authoritative teaching of Roman Catholicism.

It was this religion of authority which Freud saw as a projection of childish needs and an expression of the childish relationship to the father; while his own Jewish religion of Law influenced greatly his contention that we projected the super ego or prohibitive conscience upon God. When Flügel[1] contends that 'the most fundamental contribution of psycho-analysis to this field (religion), viz. that the attitude of man to his gods is determined to a

---

[1] 'Man, Morals and Society,' p. 261.

large extent by displacement of his attitude towards his
parents, either in their original form as dominating external figures or as incorporated in the super ego; in which
latter case there is a projection of the internal super ego
on to the external figure of God, as in the notion of the
"all-seeing eye of God" ', his statement only applies to
the two types of religion we have been considering. There
can be no question to the clinical psychologist that many
people do in fact project their prohibitive conscience upon
God and all its characteristics; their own demand for
punishment they project; the very character-structure to
restrict their pleasures in these people is really derivative
from this 'internalised conscience'. How is it possible to
think that asceticism or self-inflicted suffering can have
virtue in God's sight? To attempt to appease God is to
mistake His character wholly. In their best moments the
Old Testament prophets perceived this. The work of the
psychotherapist here is to 'attempt to purify their ideas of
God, of anger, cruelty and hatred'. It is no easy task;
indeed, if the prohibitive conscience is very strong, then, as
Flügel has remarked, 'there is a strong tendency to return
to the notion of a fierce, punishing and jealous God. So
strong is this urge that even if the metaphysical belief in
a cruel God is abandoned, the super ego often continues
to demand a standard no less severe than that which such
a God would be likely to impose'.[1]

It must not be thought that I have no use for a Religion
of Law or one of Authority. On the contrary, I believe
that the Moral Law is objective and stands over against
us as a *demand* that ought to be obeyed, and although that
demand cannot be rooted in our own desires, it is not
necessarily contrary to our desires or our biological or per-

[1] Ibid, p. 262.

sonality-needs. Moral demands are not capricious or arbitrary impositions upon our human nature. On the contrary, these demands if fulfilled are the very way to the realisation of our personality, to the expression of the image of God, the *telos,* implicit in every human being. The very essence of the moral life is that it is acquired, it is not given. All animals have the instinctive tendency to keep themselves clean; man keeps himself clean not because he has an instinctive tendency to do so, but because he learns to value the state of cleanliness which comes to him as a concept, not as a push from behind. He knows that he *ought* to keep himself in a state of cleanliness, but the *ought* is not a compulsion, but the outcome of seeing the *rightness* of it. That *ought* is the response of his conscience to what he *sees* as right. The child knows that he *must* be clean else he will be sent home from school, or sent by his mother back to the bathroom to wash his ears or the back of his neck. There is no *ought* in the child's mind because he is not old enough to appreciate the concept of the state of cleanliness .He is under *authority* which he *must* obey; the authority is external and may be rebelled against. Not so when he grows up to appreciate cleanliness; he is still under the authority, but it is the authority of his sense of rightness and beauty. Even when the adult individual is over-tired—too tired even to bother to wash his teeth before retiring—he knows that he *ought* to wash them. Whether we look at it from the point of view of authority or the Law of cleanliness, there is no arbitrary or capricious imposition upon the individual. Where the sense of ought is a response to the intuition of right there is no compulsion; the Law is felt to come from within; the authority is within oneself; in purely moral affairs, it is the authority of conscience whose authority lies in the fact that it functions on behalf of the personality as a whole.

What I think we forget is that there is an *ought* running through every sphere of the natural world. If an engineer has built a bridge and has accurately gauged the strains and stresses which the steel can bear he is able to say that the bridge *ought* to carry a certain load; if I drop an object from a high building it *ought* to fall to the ground at a certain speed. The very structure of things involves an *ought*. We may disobey that *ought* by attempting to pass over the bridge a greater weight than the strains and stresses will carry, but the bridge falls! The Laws of stresses and strains in steel are objective in the sense that they are independent of individual whims. So the moral Law is objective. Let the engineer build his bridge in consonance with the Laws of stresses and strains in steel and the bridge will do him good service; so let man build his life from his knowledge of good and evil and the following of that knowledge will bring him to his desired moral end; his authority is the authority of that knowledge and not a mere external authority that he *must* obey or bear the consequences.

I do not want to enter the vexed sphere of the relation of ethics to theology. But as a psychologist one must say that the tendency of theologians to substitute Biblical Law for the moral Law, the authority of Dogma or Church or Bible, or even God, for the authority of the moral Law tends to create those types of religion which we have been discussing and which have such direful effects upon many people. These people live in a state of perpetual insecurity, the very opposite of that which is given by a true religion; they internalise the Law; they do not assimilate it until it becomes a part of their moral nature; it stands over against

L

them with its threats if violated; it coerces them, it does not draw them. So also the authority of dogma, of Church or Bible or even God Himself is external to their personality; they comply with the demands but they do not obey. Hence the tremendous guilt they feel, the self-punishments they inflict upon themselves. There is all the difference between the man who says 'I *must* do that', and the man who says 'I *ought* to do that'; the one is in bondage, the other is free.

Those are the types of religion to which Freud's dictum applies, that 'religion is the universal obsessional neurosis'. Freud never came within sight of the religion which could say with Augustine: 'Love God and do what you like', 'We are more than conquerors', of St. Paul or, with John, 'This is the victory that overcometh the world, even our faith'.

It will not be out of place here to digress and make a comment upon the religion which psycho-analysts such as Flügel would substitute for the Christian religion, and to which Cattell's[1] theory of 'Theopsyche' gives apparent grounds. It is our old friend 'The Religion of Humanity'. Flügel[2] thinks that 'The religious emotions must be largely or entirely secularized and be put in the service of humanity. The religion of humanity is surely the religion of the near future'.

Naturally I cannot enter into a criticism of either Cattell's views or Flügel's, as I am not lecturing upon the psychology of religion. But I can ask: How far would this type of religion free us from the dangers we see in the types of religion which I have just criticised? Would it unify the personality as well as the kind of religion we shall be studying in a moment?

[1] 'Psychology and the Religious Quest.'
[2] 'Man, Morals and Society,' p. 275.

So far as the first question is concerned, the answer is firmly in the negative. Flügel must know from his clinical experience that the social sanction is as prolific of neuroses as the religion of Law or of Authority. The great majority of people who break down do so because they are afraid of the censure of society, the punishments of society, and the social consequences of giving way to their tendencies. The usual homosexual is not as a rule afraid of breaking God's Law or of disobeying the authority of God. He is afraid of society and the social ostracism which his perversion can bring him. It must not be thought for a moment that everybody who has to consult the psycho-analyst or psychotherapist is religious or makes any pretence to religion. As a matter of fact, the majority of those I have seen in thirty years' practice had no religion at all, and because they had none my task was harder. The authoritarian conscience is not necessarily a religious product. The Laws of society are far more likely to be *introjected* (to use psycho-analytic jargon) than is Biblical Law, and the authority of society is far more likely to remain external and to create guilt feelings than the authority of God. Society is there, an obvious fact to anyone, and its punishments are well known. After all, its ultimate authority is the policeman, and it has no mercy. I should far rather treat a patient whose fear of the religious sanction was the cause of his repression than one whose fear of the social sanction was the cause of his trouble.

In any case, there is no such thing as humanity, there are only particular societies. No thinker in his senses grants ultimate moral authority to any society. Society itself, in so far as it is organised into a State, acts compulsively. 'The State', as John MacMurray[1] has reminded us, 'is an

---

[1] 'Challenge to the Churches,' pp. 25 and 27.

organisation of power for the enforcement of law.' By its very nature government must rely upon fear.

If the State is to be our god—and you cannot have a society without some form of State—then as many questions as we ask about God will have to be answered. What kind of a State am I to put my emotions and energies at its service? A Bolshevik? A National-Socialistic? A Fascist? Does anyone believe that a State with a secret police or gestapo cannot create more neurosis than any kind of religion known to students? I know that we make a distinction between a *community* and a State. But can anyone outline the structure of a community which will not be based upon order, and therefore law, and therefore bound to become a State. Indeed, our safety lies in the fact that we do not allow States to be ultimates;[1] they are subject to moral Law like their citizens; they must be subject to moral criticism, for there are good States and bad States. Our salvation from neurosis does not lie there.

In regard to the second question, no one will deny that if a narrow legal and authoritarian religion is apt to produce neurosis, a surfeit of guilt feelings and a sense of moral instability, the nobler religions have produced the finest of our personalities. Not only so, but they can change the whole nature of a man's moral and spiritual life. I need not quote Professor James on conversion, that religion unifies a life which before felt divided. I am thinking of the effect of a truly spiritual religion in which the relation between God and His creature is that of the personal relationship of love. I shall not go to the theologians for a description of the advantages of religion to the human soul. I shall quote Flügel's[2] summary: 'We need not

---

[1] Cf. 'From the Human End,' by L. P. Jacks, Essay on 'The State as the Sterilizer of Virtue.'
[2] 'Man, Morals and Society,' p. 268.

feel that we are weak and helpless puppets of Chance or Destiny, forlorn orphans in a vast, heedless universe; on the contrary, we can enjoy the sense of playing an important part in a scheme of things run by an omnipotent Creator who watches over us lovingly as we play the rôle He has allotted to us. Our puny efforts acquire dignity and meaning as part of a Higher Purpose. The seeming hardships and injustices of life lose their sting when we believe that they only appear to us in this light because of the shortness of our vision, or at least that divine justice will recompense us amply for the sufferings we have endured. When belief in personal immortality is added to our belief in God, the ever-present threat of death loses its horror when confronted with the prospect of bliss. Finally, our intellectual curiosity is gratified by an explanation of the origin, nature and purpose of the universe so far as our limited intellects are capable of grasping problems of this magnitude, and our moral perplexities can be resolved with a minimum of trouble or conflict by a reference to the Divine Will in so far as this has been made manifest to us'.

Flügel is not astonished at the attractions of all this and that men grasp eagerly these advantages. 'We need hardly wonder that men grasp eagerly at the "illusion".'

Actually the advantages are far more than this. From the purely psychological point of view it does not matter whether it is an 'illusion' or not—that is a question for the philosopher and not the psychologist. But from the purely psychological point of view can anyone imagine a system of beliefs more likely to unify the personality and give stability to the whole psychological life than those advantages which Flügel outlines?

Add to those advantages the undoubted capacity of

religion to dissipate guilt feelings, to make an individual at one with himself, with his fellows and with whatever he believes to be behind this universe, and above all to reveal him to himself by opening the door between conscious and unconscious, and we need not be surprised at the tremendous functional value of religion which Freud has to acknowledge. Naturally the theologian cannot be satisfied with a functional view of religion; his question is not whether it does this or that, but is it true? Even the psychologist, however, cannot but wonder whether religion could have this great functional value unless it had a basis in reality.

What I want to emphasise from this long digression is that although the wrong type of religion can be a breeding place for neurosis, it does not follow that all religion is an obsessional neurosis or any kind of neurosis, A neurosis means that the personality is divided against itself. Religion unifies; it can create a new individual in a new world; it can give a new habitual centre from which to act, to think and to feel. If the sense of belonging, as Erich Fromm contends, is vital to a mind free from basic anxiety, then religion, above all else, can give this sense of belonging to One Whom we can absolutely trust. The 'peace of God that passeth all understanding' is no illusory figment of the imagination, else I have been living under this 'illusion' for over fifty years. That peace is the emotional tone of a state of mind which is a 'harmony of experience with feeling'. Conscience, reason, emotion and behaviour tendencies are working in harmony to give that peace.

No one knows better than the clinical psychologists that the conflicts characteristic of nervous breakdown are not different from those which precede a conversion. There is the same sense of division, often an extreme sense of guilt, the sense of alienation, often a feeling of despair and hope-lessness. The neurotic's symptoms are the outcome of re-pression; he has escaped his conflicts by an escape into psychological illness; his conflicts remain unresolved. The feelings which precede a religious decision or conversion are the outcome of an awakening to the meaning of the conflicts within the individual's mind; there is a struggle between the inclinations and the will; there is a deep sense of the moral implications of the conflicts. The decision or the conversion is the sign that the conflicts have been faced in consciousness, and with the repentance, involving both sorrow and the turning of the whole personality towards God, the conflicts are resolved; the divided self is unified.

It is well then to remember that the religious sentiment, like all other sentiments, is an organisation of impulse, behaviour-tendencies, ideas and emotions round the idea or object of the sentiment. In this case the organisation is round the idea of God. That is the vital thing. If the idea of God is juridical, authoritarian or narrow, then the sentiment will be rooted in infantile reactions and the pro-hibitive conscience. We call the result 'religion', but it will be religion at a 'low temperature', and its personalities will be gaunt and starved, sometimes fanatical even if they have been able to evade a neurosis. 'The glorification of power', writes Whitehead[1] (and he might have added Law), 'has broken more hearts than it has healed.'

It must not be thought for a moment that the severity of the religious sanction or the social sanction is responsible for all the neurosis in modern life. On the contrary, the lack of any religion or attachment to society is one of the most prolific causes of breakdown. These people may be all right until they come up against some strong tempta-

[1] 'Religion in the Making.'

tion, or some unexpected bereavement, or a change in their economic circumstances, and then they crack. They have no spiritual resources, no reserves of moral strength on which they can fall back, no philosophy or religion that could give some kind of meaning to the contradiction they have now to meet at the hands of life.

In my last Tate lectures I dealt with the need for a philosophy of life and contended that for most people their philosophy of life is contained in their religious beliefs. I do not doubt for a moment that a philosophy of life which has no religious basis whatsoever can provide a stable background to life in spite of the fact that we have no answer to the string of questions that Lord Russell tells us that philosophy asks. We can remain ignorant of many things without our emotional balance being disturbed. Lord Russell[1] goes further and tells us that philosophy has for part of its function to help us to live in spite of that uncertainty. 'Uncertainty', he tells us, 'in the presence of vivid hopes and fears, is painful, but must be endured if we wish to live without the support of comforting fairy tales. It is not good either to forget the questions that philosophy asks, or to persuade ourselves that we have found indubitable answers to them. To teach how to live without certainty, and yet without being paralysed by hesitation, is perhaps the chief thing that philosophy, in our age, can still do for those who study it.' Here, as Principal Cross[2] pointed out in a brilliant critical appreciation of Lord Russell's *History of Western Philosophy*, is really the task of religious faith, and surreptitiously Lord Russell is ascribing to philosophy what is actually the

[1] 'History of Western Philosophy,' p. 11. (London: George Allen & Unwin Ltd.)

[2] 'Hibbert Journal,' April, 1947.

function of faith. Unfortunately, that brilliant philosopher has never realised that theological dogma (his fairy tales) is not identical with religious faith. A man may have a strong religious faith or at least faith without being very certain about any dogmas. Paul does not say that we live by dogmas, but that *The Just shall live by faith.* Alas! our Reformers, following in the wake of the dogmatism of Medieval Catholicism, made that into a dogma by giving a theological content to faith, and by insisting that certain dogmas must be believed before we could have faith. Psychologically there are no beliefs that *must be believed.* Immediately we lay down certain beliefs as *must* be believed we are sowing the seeds of a compulsion neurosis and not the foundation of a faith.

It would not be difficult to prove that the stable background to a man's soul which a philosophy can give is the outcome of faith and not of his particular beliefs or certainty. We may believe dogmas without having any faith, for faith is not a mere assent to propositions to whose grounds we have no access; and we may have faith with a very minimum of certainty of belief. Faith cannot but seek grounds for itself, but it is not the grounds of faith that give the certainty; that is the function of faith itself. We shall see later that faith *is* knowledge, that it brings us into the presence of the object, and this knowledge gives certitude.

That a fine, vital religion does not depend on dogma, let me quote the experience of Dr. Estlin Carpenter,[1] a saint if ever there was one. Writing to a friend who was greatly troubled about religious dogmas, he says: 'I was in a condition of religious apathy for a long time when at Manchester College, Oxford. I had no intellectual doubts; I

[1] 'Life of J. E. Carpenter,' p. 10.

do not think I am able to entertain them; that means,
perhaps, that I had not departed from the philosophy in
which I had been trained. But though I had no doubts, I
had no religion. I had no sense of personal relationship
to God. I never wished particularly to pray. I hoped that
if I went for a time to work among the poor and ignorant
my religion might in some way be renewed in me. It was
brought about in this way. Dr. Martineau persuaded me
to wait in college, and one summer I went to stay with
Wicksteed at his father's house in North Wales. Shall I
tell you what happened? . . . I went out one afternoon
for a walk, alone. I was in that empty, unthinking state
in which one saunters along country lanes, simply yield-
ing oneself to the casual sights and sounds. . . . Suddenly I
was conscious of the presence of someone else. I cannot
describe it, but I felt that I had a direct perception of the
Being of God all around me. It came unsought and absolutely unexpectedly. The experience did not last long, but
it sufficed to change my whole being. This event has never
happened to me again. It was not necessary. There are
some things which when a man has grasped them, he can
not let them go'.

Here is faith as knowledge; he is ushered into the
presence of the Object, and not merely a 'faith in someone else's faith'. Meaning came into his life at that
moment, the sense of isolation was taken away, he experienced a status that his philosophy could not give him,
a love and sense of security that stood him in good stead
when he came to suffer some hard contradictions at the
hands of life. It was that experience that created the belief
that the same experience could have come to the members
of other religions. It was the inspiration of all the goodness and service so manifest in that life. There was no

dogma given in that revelation; faith was born without dogma. Psychologically, revelation is never a revelation of dogma. The revelation of forgiveness does not give us the dogma of atonement; the revelation of The Holy Spirit's reality does not give us the dogma of the Trinity; the revelation that God was in Christ does not give us a dogma of Incarnation. The man whose religion is dependent wholly on dogma is like 'a bee trying to suck honey from a wilted flower'.

Faith cannot help but seek grounds for itself. But that is true of every experience, sensory as well as emotional and spiritual. The fault lies in identifying our faith with certain propositions. What Lord Russell[1] says about philosophy can be said about religion. He writes: 'Ever since men became capable of free speculation, their actions, in innumerable important respects, have depended upon their theories as to the world and human life, as to what is good and what is evil. This is as true in the present day as at any former time. . . . There is here reciprocal causation: the circumstances of men's lives do much to determine their philosophy, but, conversely, their philosophy does much to determine their circumstances'. So with religion, the content of the idea of God, of His relationship towards us, what He is supposed to condemn as evil and approve as good, determines the kind of religious experience the individual is likely to have. And especially is this true of the morbid religious experiences, such as the guilt and anxiety we have been studying. On the other hand, the kind of life one is seeking to live, the spirit of our life, can and does modify both the influences the dogmas, taught us in our youth, have upon us, and the

[1] 'History of Western Philosophy,' p. 11. (London: George Allen & Unwin Ltd.)

dogmas themselves. I do not doubt that it is the calmness, the peace and sense of security, the feeling that life has meaning, which came to Dr. Carpenter in that experience of the Presence which elicits the intuition that the Being Who revealed Himself in the experience is Love.

What kind of religion, then, from the psychological view is likely to give that kind of certitude amid all the uncertainty of our knowledge of ultimate things and of life itself which keeps the soul stable and free from all the debilitating conflicts which characterise our age? And how does religion mediate her gifts? These are the two questions that remain to be answered.

Perhaps the best way to answer the first question is to ask what needs man has, to which religion is always an ingredient in their full satisfaction.

Actually there is no personality-need in which religion is not involved in its realisation. The whole which the self is ever consciously or unconsciously striving to achieve is not an isolated self-sufficient whole. Its wholeness is realised in relation to others, in fellowship with others, in personal relation with others; in a word, it is achieved in a community. There is no happiness outside personal relations, and all nervous breakdown of a neurotic kind is a disturbance of personal relations. There must be a sharing of the life of others—a sharing of their sorrows as well as their joys, their struggles as well as achievements. Indeed, I should go further and say that the very highest good in seeking which we realise our ethical wholeness is THE SEEKING OF THE THINGS WHICH GAIN BY BEING SHARED. However we characterise the Kingdom of God, will it not be a community in which all are sharing the things which gain by being shared, and all motivated by the desire to seek the things which gain by being shared.

I wish I had space to develop this in relation to the ethical doctrine of The Common Good. Every neurotic patient has to surrender his ego-centricity and gain object-centricity. Every degree of ego-centricity he surrenders, his mental health returns to that degree; and every degree of object-centricity the normal man gains, to that degree he is proof against the mental conflicts which can deprive him of peace of mind.

The drive for wholeness cannot stop with the community. We live and move and have our being in the Whole we call the universe; and no individual whose need for rational and moral unity has a chance to function can help asking what his relation to that universe is and what is its relation to him. No man can be said to have grown up who has never sought to find out his relationship to whatever lies behind the universe. In other words, he must seek for a meaning to his own life, whether it has any purpose transcending himself, his loved ones and community. He may come to a negative position; he may accept a materialistic philosophy and see in the universe no spiritual meaning whatsoever. At least he knows where he stands, and he lives his life accordingly. He does not live from hand to mouth as one must live who has never asked those questions.. He may, on the other hand, root his life in the religious ideas which he has received as a child and, in so far as these ideas are not cutting across his biological or personality-needs, they will give him guidance. They may, as Mannheim[1] has suggested, provide the paradigms with which his religious experiences will accord. That drive for wholeness may be blocked by sincere intellectual doubts, or by the contradictions one sees in modern life, or by the failure to discern any purpose in history

[1] 'Diagnosis of Our Times,' pp. 135—139.

or significance in his own life. Such doubts do not lead to
neurosis or even conflicts of a distressing kind. There can
be no doubt, however, that they do lead to a depressing
sense of utter insignificance and hopelessness which can
take a great deal of the zest from living. This sense of insignificance was a common theme at the end of the last
century and the beginning of this. In face of the vast
forces which science was discovering, the insignificance of
our little earth with the vast accumulation of space, men
felt that they were less significant than a speck of dust.
The sense of insignificance today is generated by forces
that impinge upon our lives much more closely than any
of the concepts which depressed our grandfathers. The
growing possibility of being governed by ideologies against
which the individual must fight in vain, the up-surge of
bestial elements which were by no means exhausted by
the concentration camps of Germany, the growing gulf between East and West in politics which ultimately can mean
war in which whole populations will be at the mercy of
the atom bomb, and the very little any one individual can
do to save the situation is at the root of a great deal of
depression today. Economic incentives are at a low ebb,
and our standards of living seem to be at the mercy of
economic forces over which we appear to have little control. All this is generating a new sense of hopelessness and
insignificance which is being expressed in literature as an
ever-recurring theme, according to Desmond MacCarthy
of the *Sunday Times*. One writer whose essay he was re-
viewing expresses the feeling as 'like a melancholy sprat
being caught up in the Niagara Falls'. Compensation for
this insignificance and hopelessness is afforded by phantasy
islands and dreams. Our writers are seeking a refuge. This
is how Desmond MacCarthy puts it: 'The island is

evidently a projection of the longing for religion and the sweet security of childhood (the two often combine in sensitive natures). For religion is the surest cure for all that feeling of personal insignificance which afflicts so many today. In a weltering world it offers one permanent relation to ephemeral atoms who may die by the million without making more than a minute temporary difference to the course things will take—their relation to God in which what they are and what they do is still of significance, even lasting significance. Religion bridges the ludicrous gulf between the instinctive sense of significance imposed by consciousness itself—each of us being a centre of his world and what we know to be the true sense of proportion'.

From this we see that the conditions of modern life are not only cutting across the drive for wholeness, for a harmony between experience and feeling, but across our need for status. Read 'status' for 'significance' in the quotation from Desmond MacCarthy, and you have my point.

Religious faith alone is the way out of the present condition of hopelessness, for religion alone links us with the Whole which philosophers call Reality, and only in personal relationship with that Reality can life be experienced as a Whole. Psychologically, religion is the way to wholeness.

Already I have hinted in the quotation from MacCarthy that religion is an ingredient in the realisation of the fundamental need for Status. 'We are children of God', says John, 'co-heirs with Christ', Paul echoes. What that has meant in individual lives every psychologist knows. It meant self-respect, a sense of dignity, a sense of purpose; and these are the very things which underlie all mental health. In our depersonalised world the individual becomes less and less. Is it not a tragedy that in our modern world it is only in war that the individual regains his status? In war we live to work; in peace we are reduced to beings who just work to live—there is no more ultimate meaning to our work, and the mere economic rewards do not satisfy the soul of man. The great majority carry on, but the deep fundamental personality-needs whose satisfaction give life are unsatisfied. Give work a religious meaning, and however lowly it may be, it is expressing our personality; we are 'co-labourers with God'.

Nor must the philosopher forget that religion gives what philosophy cannot give; it gives *ontological status* to the individual. It was that ontological status that motivated our fathers' fight for freedom, justice and the right to believe. From one point of view the 'Clue to History' is man's struggle to maintain his status as a spiritual being against tyrannies, political and economic, which denied him or would have taken from him that status. Apart from the ontological status which religion gives the individual there is no more reason why the strong should not tyrannise over the weak than there is for the tiger to lie down with the lamb.[1]

As it is with the need for wholeness, rational and moral unity, and status, so it is with the need for affection. Granted that many people's religion is of a childish nature, and that their love to God is a neurotic love, ego-centric and selfish, can anyone deny that religion more than any other appeal or experience can elicit the purest object-centred love to God and to man? Probably the most difficult command to obey in the New Testament is: Love thy neighbour as thyself. To love people is very hard and few there be who can do it. Those few are those who love

[1] See quotation in 'God's Grace and Man's Hopes,' by Williams, pp. 184 and 185.

God with mind, heart and soul. They love people because God loves them and because they see even the most debased as God's children. That relationship of love to God which feeds their own soul and motivates their love to man is an experience as real as that of sense perception. It is the psychological reality of that relationship of love to God elicited by the knowledge of God's love to them that underlies the sense of status, the sense of rational and moral unity experienced by the truly religious individual.

I need not repeat how religion dissipates the sense of guilt, transforms our sense of shame and humiliation into repentance, and gives us that fundamental trust in the faithfulness of God through which we stand four-square to all the storms which life can bring.

Yes, we may say that all this is built on 'fairy tales', that the religious objects are 'illusions'; what matters is that the experience is not an illusion nor a fairy tale; it is psychological fact. These experiences, as Jung has well pointed out, do not establish dogmas or doctrine; they are the starting point for both. To quote Jung: 'Religious experience is absolute. It is indisputable. You can only say that you have never had such an experience, and your opponent will say: "Sorry, I have". And there your discussion will come to an end. No matter what the world thinks about religious experience, the one who has it possesses the great treasure of a thing that has provided him with the source of life, meaning and beauty, and that has given a new splendour to the world and mankind. He has pistis (Faith) and peace. . . . Nobody can know what the ultimate things are. We must, therefore, take them as we experience them. And if such experience helps to make your life healthier, more beautiful, more complete, and

[1] 'Religion and Psychology,' p. 50.

M

more satisfactory to yourself and to those you love, you may safely say: "This was the grace of God" '.[1]

The integrated life, the realisation of the life as a self-conscious whole in personal love relations with others and God, the realising of the *telos,* the image of God within us—this is what religious experience gives us. That experience is the enjoyment of God, the sharing of the life of God. We have fellowship with God in the simple offices of praise, prayer and meditation, but also we have fellowship with Him in sharing the suffering of the world, in the creative and redemptive process—we fill up the sufferings left behind—in beauty, goodness and truth. In seeking first the Kingdom of God we have a comprehensive end in which all our powers can be engaged.

Finally, how does religion mediate her gifts? The answer is through Faith.

It is doubtful whether psychology has yet brought out all the meaning of religious faith. Faith is still too closely allied to the idea of submission to authority, to the acceptance of dogma, and to the acceptance of propositions to whose grounds we have no access. Too often we have attempted an analogy with the 'faith' we are supposed to have to exercise every day in life in order to live; or we have likened it to the faith of the scientist in the Uniformity of Nature. I myself have been guilty of this fallacy. Actually we can only have faith in persons. When I say that I have faith in the strength of a lift to take me to the top floor of a building safely, I am not exercising faith, but tacitly trusting in the calculus of probabilities. Faith is an experience of the supersensuous; we are in the presence of the object, although the object is unseen. Dr. Carpenter's experience of God was the evidence of the unseen. Our experience of forgiveness, of God's presence or His love, of *actual* grace that comes in answer to our need, are immediate experiences; none of these is an inference. Immediate experience, writes Whitehead, is infallible. It is when we attempt to embody our experience in abstract propositions that error arises. It is the imposition of these abstract propositions on our children that do the damage which I have lamented in these lectures. Inevitably these abstract propositions form particular patterns of belief and patterns of behaviour. When we attempt to impose patterns of belief or behaviour we forget the fact of individuality. We fall into the same fallacy as those psychologists who talk as though there were mind in general, persons in general, when there is no such thing. There are just individuals expressing all the variety of their individuality. So in the religious life; there is a variety of religious experience.

Faith is knowledge coming to us through a direct encounter with God. The particular encounter with God will depend very largely on the need that is driving us: one man is driven by his sense of guilt, his weakness in face of sin or moral conflict; another is moved by the loss of his religious inspiration as Dr. Carpenter was; while still another is driven to seek for some meaning to history amid its bewildering contradictions; still another by the need to find some kind of ultimate values in life. One may not be ostensibly seeking for God, although I think that subconsciously each one of us in virtue of the religious training of our youth is implicitly feeling after Him as the way through our problems or the satisfaction of the need. The *quality*, not the quantity, of our striving, I believe, is a determining factor in the particular revelation of God to which our faith is the response. The neurotic is only concerned to get rid of his guilt; he is not seeking God in spite of the number and intensity of his prayers. The unconscious religious rebel in spite of his apparent diligence in reading and discussion is not seeking for a resolution of his religious doubts; unconsciously he is pre-occupied with the problem as to how he can answer his religious opponents. Any psychologist can discern a good deal of this in the writings of Lord Russell, who never misses an opportunity to gibe at religious beliefs, especially if they are Christian. Once the neurotic is brought to realise that his concern should not be about the guilt and fear but the behaviour tendencies which have caused him to feel guilty, he is near the moment when faith will be born in a response to the grace of God. A certain moral state is invariably found to correlate with the birth or response of faith. (True faith) 'is not born accidently, from circumstances or traditions: it is not born of a factitious enthusiasm or an intellectual effort: nor is it born of the caprice or the despair of the will. It is born in the revelation of the object; and that revelation is the fruit—I dare not call it the reward—of steadfast moral toil'.[1] That is borne out in every sphere in which God reveals Himself. It is not uncommon for those under the 'conviction of sin' at revival meetings or during a time of revival to be under that conviction for days struggling to 'let the light in', or to surrender to the Holy Object revealed; and then as suddenly and in spite of their conscious struggles, as unexpectedly as Dr. Carpenter, they know they are forgiven, released from the sense of guilt, 'saved', as they put it. There is a great deal in the contention of Professor Frommel[2]: 'This response of man to the Divine action which seeks him in his con-

---

[1] 'The Psychology of Christian Faith,' by Professor Frommel, p. 131 f.
[2] Ibid, p. 132.

science is what we properly mean by faith. Belief in God has always meant, and will always mean, responding practically to the initiative of God in conscience'. The striving that finds its fruit in faith has always a moral element; and it always brings us into the presence of the object of faith. Actually I think it will be found that in many cases it is when the struggle ceases that the revelation comes.

So far I have been speaking of religious faith. Earlier I spoke of the philosopher living by faith. That is true. No philosopher can prove that there is a moral element in Reality corresponding to our sense of ought; in other words, that the moral law is objective. Our sense of 'ought' brings us into the presence of that moral element in Reality. So with Beauty, and with Truth. These ultimate values are mediated to us through faith. Some thinkers would even go further and contend that we never get outside ourselves—our perceptions, our feelings, our thoughts, and consequently no proof can be given that our sense perceptions are in real contact with an external object that corresponds to those sense-perceptions. An unconscious act of faith gives us the assurance of the object.

Be that as it may, it has always been the contention of the Church that Faith is the medium of God's grace, and indeed is the beginning of the Christian life. That faith is the response of the self, the subject, the spirit to the living presence of God. 'It is the breaking of the shell of self-centredness and the free commitment of the self to the power and goodness of God. Faith is more than belief, though it involves belief. Faith is more than an act of will, though it involves a decision of the will. Faith is response. It is the whole-souled giving of life into the keeping of

God, who is the absolutely trustworthy source and re-
deemer of life.'[1]

Faith always involves commitment, for on psychological analysis faith is always found to be incipient action
to that commitment; on the negative side faith tends to
exert an inhibition on anything that would hinder the
commitment.

Once that commitment is made there comes trust—the
feeling that goes out to the object of faith—and confidence
—the inner feeling of security which banishes the basic
anxiety of which Karen Horney speaks.

Here we find the fundamental weakness of the neurotic
—he cannot commit himself. Brow-beaten by his sense of
guilt, terrorised by his infantile prohibitive conscience, he
is afraid even to allow the offending behaviour-tendencies
to come into consciousness. He has lost confidence in his
power to control them, and cannot trust God to give him
the power. Hence his unconscious repression of the tendencies. The whole work of the Christian psychologist here
is plain. Gradually he helps to reduce the intolerance and
harshness of the infantile conscience by introducing the
positive conscience which without fear can condemn the
offending tendencies and bring them under guidance. When
the guilt is attached to the tendencies and not to the
neurotic-fear-objects, forgiveness can be found and the
whole series of personal relations which had been disturbed
restored. The capacity to see themselves, that is to say to
allow the unconscious to become conscious without panick-
ing, is steadily developed, and the whole of their tendencies
become integrated with the conscious adult personality.
They begin to 'grow in grace', they get a sense of security.
or, as our fathers would have said, they get assurance.
Like St. Paul they can say: 'I know whom I have believed

[1] 'God's Grace and Man's Hope.' p. 187.

and am persuaded that He is able to keep that which I have committed unto Him'.

Without that religious assurance and faith the neurotic is always in danger of relapsing. We may alleviate his fears, we may reduce the intolerance of his prohibitive conscience, we may help to lift the repression so that his behaviour-tendencies are able to come into consciousness. If, however, he begins to play with self-indulgence and gives way, the repression may become very severe and the harshness of his prohibitive conscience increased tenfold.

When religion enters into the cure there is a true turning of the whole self, not only towards God, but towards the service of others through the Church, or through one or other of the many organisations that serve the common good. Instead now of being afraid to be bad, they are turned toward a life of Good. They come to love good more than they hate evil; they love the good more than they fear the wrong. That is where their safety lies. A true religion that is found in sharing the life of God, in the enjoyment of God, which is a real love response to God, is the best preventive of neurosis; and the one real guarantee of its cure. That is so because the *telos* of our being is the image of God, and in fellowship with God and co-operation with God's children, the dynamic urge of that image finds its object.